Fish Out Of W...

A Comedy

Derek Benfield

Samuel French – London
New York – Sydney – Toronto – Hollywood

FISH OUT OF WATER

Presented by Michael Ward, in association with the Horseshoe Theatre Company, on a national tour which opened at the Haymarket Theatre, Basingstoke, on April 3rd 1986, with the following cast of characters:

Audrey Hubback	Beth Ellis
Marisa	Rena Jugati
Brigadier Hubback	Trevor Bannister
Agatha Hepworth	Jane Freeman
Fiona Francis	Jennifer Wilson
Julian Whittle	Nick Field
Mario Marcello	Clive Flint

The play directed by **Charles Savage**
Setting by **John Page**

It all happens in a sun-drenched hotel on the Italian Riviera at the height of the summer season

ACT I   Scene 1 Afternoon
        Scene 2 Early the same evening

ACT II Scene 1 The following morning
        Scene 2 The same evening

Time—the present

This is a new version of the play that was first produced at the New Theatre, Bromley, on April 2nd, 1962, and was first published in 1963.

Also by Derek Benfield

Touch and Go
Look Who's Talking!
Beyond a Joke
Caught on the Hop
In for the Kill
Panic Stations
A Bird in the Hand
Murder for the Asking
Post Horn Gallop
Off the Hook!
Running Riot
Wild Goose Chase

ACT I

The lounge of a hotel on the Italian Riviera. The sun is scorching down. A summer afternoon

In the lounge two wide steps lead to large, open glass doors which open out to the swimming-pool and hotel gardens, with potted plants on the patio and purple bougainvillaea cascading profusely outside the windows. A staircase UC leads up to the bedrooms and there is an archway UL opening into the entrance hall, with vivid holiday posters on the wall

The lounge is furnished with two comfortable armchairs, one DL and one DR; two sofas, one against the wall between the stairs and the glass doors, and the other above a low coffee-table DLC. There is another low table with two smaller armchairs DRC, and a built-in padded seat in the corner above the archway. Three small tables, each with a practical lamp, and various cheerful, colourful paintings on the walls complete the furnishings. The decoration is bright and summery

It is peaceful and hot, with only the distant rattle of the cicadas in the trees outside

When the CURTAIN rises Audrey Hubback, a rather severe, upper-class woman of about fifty, is apparently asleep on the sofa DL, an open book on her lap

Pause

Marisa, a strikingly pretty Italian girl with everything in the right place, enters down the stairs. She is in a very brief bikini and carries a beach towel. She walks across the lounge and exits through the glass doors leading to the swimming-pool

   No sooner has she gone than Brigadier Hubback comes down the stairs quickly, obviously in pursuit. He is a jovial, well-preserved, ex-Army officer in his middle fifties. From his neck hangs a pair of binoculars. He does not see his sleeping wife and makes, enthusiastically, for the glass doors in pursuit of Marisa

But his wife, of course, is not asleep

Mrs Hubback Charles!

Hubback stops, furtively

Hubback Good lord! I didn't know *you* were there!

Mrs Hubback Where are you going?

Hubback (*nervously*) Am I going somewhere?

Mrs Hubback You *appeared* to be going somewhere.

Hubback Ah. Yes. I—I was going there.

Mrs Hubback Going where?

Hubback (*indicating*) Through there.

Mrs Hubback Why?

Hubback What?

Mrs Hubback Why were you going through there?

Hubback Yes.

Mrs Hubback What?

Hubback To the beach. Have a swim.

Mrs Hubback You don't appear to be dressed for aquatics.

Hubback Don't I?

Mrs Hubback Well, that doesn't look to *me* like bathing trunks. More like a
   suit.

Hubback Yes. It's a bathing suit.

Mrs Hubback Don't be idiotic!

Hubback Underneath!

Mrs Hubback What?

Hubback My bathing trunks. They're underneath.

Mrs Hubback (*appalled*) You surely don't intend to strip on the sands?

Hubback Er—well, I . . .

Mrs Hubback Leave your suit in a bundle on the beach? You're a brigadier
   on a holiday to Italy, not a piano-tuner on a day trip to Ilfracombe!

Hubback Yes. Yes, that's true. I don't play the piano. Never learned as a
   kid. (*Thoughtfully*) Too busy marching, I suppose . . . I'll go and change.
   (*He tries to escape*)

Mrs Hubback Furtive!

Hubback (*stopping*) What?

Mrs Hubback If you ask me.

Hubback Ask you what?

Mrs Hubback What you are! That's what I'd say. Very furtive.

Hubback Me?

Mrs Hubback You!

Hubback Never!

Mrs Hubback You were creeping about like a guilty man. (*She eyes him
   suspiciously*) You're *not* a guilty man, are you?

Hubback (*stammering nervously*) N-n-n-n-n-no! No, of course not. Not
   guilty. Never. No. If I'd known you were there I'd . . .

Mrs Hubback Have been more careful?

Hubback Exactly! (*Quickly*) No! Not exactly *careful*. I thought you were
   upstairs asleep.

Mrs Hubback Well, I wasn't. I was down here—with all my wits about me.

Hubback You *said* you were going to sleep. So I assumed—naturally—that
   you'd be sleeping upstairs.

Mrs Hubback You assumed wrongly.

Hubback Apparently.

Mrs Hubback When you were in the Army I hope you made better assumptions on the field of battle.

Hubback Certainly! You don't become a brigadier by bungling.

Mrs Hubback I wouldn't be too sure about that. (*She glares at him*)

Hubback (*edging towards the glass doors*) Well, I . . . I think I'll go and sit in the sun.

Mrs Hubback It's far too hot for that!

Hubback Is it?

Mrs Hubback Certainly. You'd burst into flames like a bundle of sticks.

Hubback (*sulking*) I would like to get a bit more sun-tanned before we go back home.

Mrs Hubback (*snorting*) Huh! Not much chance of that.

Hubback Getting sun-tanned?

Mrs Hubback Going home. Not much chance of going home.

Hubback Not even tomorrow?

Mrs Hubback (*looking at him wearily*) Don't you *ever* read the newspapers? You've heard of baggage handlers!

Hubback Have I?

Mrs Hubback Baggage handlers! At the airport!

Hubback Oh, *that* baggage. Yes.

Mrs Hubback Well, they're not.

Hubback Not?

Mrs Hubback Handling the baggage! Not as quickly as they might. At this time of year it's a wonder any planes get off the ground at all.

Hubback (*hopefully*) Ah! So we could be delayed even longer?

Mrs Hubback More than likely.

Hubback Oh, splendid! That'll give me a bit more time. (*He looks towards the pool with a smile*)

Mrs Hubback (*suspiciously*) Time for what?

Hubback To sun in the sit. Er—sit in the sun!

Mrs Hubback (*giving a long-suffering look*) Oh, for heaven's sake come over here.

Hubback (*gloomily*) Not very sunny over there . . .

Mrs Hubback That's the idea. This is siesta time. In this climate all sensible people sleep for a while in the afternoon. It's far too hot out there. Especially for you.

Hubback What do you mean?

Mrs Hubback At your age something might happen to you.

Hubback I wish it would! (*He looks longingly out of the glass doors*)

Mrs Hubback What *you* need is a cup of tea. Where's that girl got to?

Hubback (*without thinking*) She's out there. (*He looks smilingly out towards the pool*)

Mrs Hubback What?

Hubback (*covering quickly*) She's probably out there. Or out there—(*he waves vaguely in the other direction*)—or somewhere. Probably. Yes.

Mrs Hubback If you ask me it's more than tea you want.

Hubback Yes, it certainly is!

Marisa enters through the glass-doors, a little breathless, drying herself on her towel

Marisa Oh, it is so wonderful out there!

Hubback (*to his wife*) You see? What did I tell you?

Mrs Hubback It may be all right for her. She *lives* in Italy. She's used to it. It's not quite the same thing for you, Charles.

Marisa I always think the afternoon is the best time to do it.

Hubback (*grinning*) Yes, so do I!

Mrs Hubback Charles!

Hubback (*hastily miming the breast stroke*) To swim! The best time to swim!

Marisa The pool was so warm and so empty I did not need a bathing suit.

Hubback (*goggling at the thought*) You mean you—er—you actually—er—— Oh, my God——!

Marisa It was all right. There was nobody there to see me.

Hubback (*ruefully*) No—they were all inside having a bloody siesta!

Mrs Hubback I really don't know what's the matter with you. The temperature goes above eighty and you become quite impossible.

Marisa (*smiling cosily at Hubback*) Would you dry my back, please, Charlie?

Hubback looks pleased. His wife does not

Hubback Oh, yes—rather! (*He starts to dry her back*)

Mrs Hubback (*coldly*) Charles——

Hubback Only trying to help—— (*He shrugs helplessly at Marisa and hands the towel back to her*)

Marisa proceeds to dry herself rather vigorously, with somewhat distracting results for Hubback

Mrs Hubback (*patiently*) Marisa, I should like some tea.

Marisa Yes. Of course. I will see to it at once.

Hubback (*coldly*) Thank you.

Marisa pulls a face at Hubback

Hubback Any new arrivals due today, Marisa?

Marisa Oh, yes. But they are already late. There have been long delays at the airports in England.

Hubback (*knowledgeably*) Yes. I know. Baggage handlers.

Mrs Hubback gives her husband a look

We were due to leave today but we've been delayed until tomorrow morning, so——(*with heavy innuendo*) we've got an extra night.

Marisa That is very nice for you.

Hubback (*beaming at her*) Yes, it certainly is!

Mrs Hubback (*wearily*) Charles——

Marisa I will get your tea.

Mrs Hubback I was afraid you'd forgotten.

As Marisa passes Hubback she gives him a friendly pinch on the bottom. He reacts with surprise and delight

Hubback Aah!

Marisa grins and exits through the arch

Mrs Hubback Whatever's the matter?

Hubback What?

Mrs Hubback You called out.

Hubback Ah. Yes. I ... I had a sudden pain.

Mrs Hubback Pain? Sounded more like pleasure.

Hubback (*enthusiastically*) Yes, it was!

Mrs Hubback What?

Hubback Er—the sun!

Mrs Hubback The *sun*?

Hubback You know what the sun is.

Mrs Hubback Of course I know what the sun is. But why should the sun cause you pain?

Hubback Well, you see, it ... it suddenly came through that window and ... and pinched me on the bottom.

Mrs Hubback What?

Hubback On the neck! Shone on the neck. *This* neck. And it was very hot. Very hot indeed. About ninety degrees, I should think. And that's why I called out.

Mrs Hubback looks at him, witheringly

Mrs Hubback Don't be so stupid.

Hubback No. Right.

Mrs Hubback That girl goes much too far.

Hubback (*quietly*) I wish she *would* ...

Mrs Hubback Calling you Charlie.

Hubback (*smiling*) Yes, it *was* rather nice, wasn't it? (*He hastily rearranges his face*) Yes, much too far! (*He drifts away*)

Mrs Hubback I shall have to speak to the manager about her.

Hubback No, no! I'll speak to her. The manager's far too busy. So many guests at this time of year.

Mrs Hubback And more arriving any minute.

Hubback Absolutely!

Mrs Hubback Heaven alone knows where they're going to put them all. The situation will soon become impossible.

Hubback I always love to see the new lot arrive, don't you? (*He chuckles*) All white and sheepish, creeping in as if they'd no right to be here! Hardly speak above a whisper.

But, at that moment, Agatha Hepworth comes in from the hall, bursting with exuberant self-confidence. She is a loud, cheerful, middle-aged woman. She is carrying a small suitcase, her handbag and a duty-free bag and is positively beaming with joy

Agatha Here! *You!*

The Hubbacks look at her, aghast

This the Hotel Floreat?

Hubback (*apprehensively*) Er—yes, it is.

Agatha bellows at someone outside

Agatha All right, Fiona! This is it! (*She advances into the room, beaming with delight. As she reaches Hubback she hands her case and duty-free bag to him, and looks about, taking in her new surroundings with obvious delight*) Ooh, it's *lovely*, isn't it? Just like the picture in the brotcher. (*She waves to Mrs Hubback*) Hullo there, dear! You all right?

Agatha turns back to Hubback who is standing very still, holding the luggage

There's some more of those outside.

Hubback (*dazed*) Oh, good. I'll be glad of some more.

Agatha (*crossing, chattily, to Mrs Hubback*) We thought we were never going to get off, you know.

Mrs Hubback (*coolly*) Really?

Agatha Oh, yes. There's some sort of a dispute going on. Well, there always is at this time of the year, isn't there? It's either air traffic control or lavatory cleaners.

Hubback Baggage!

Agatha I beg your pardon?

Hubback That's what it is. Baggage handlers.

Agatha Oh, really? Anyhow, our plane was late taking off. (*She smiles enthusiastically*) Five whole extra hours at the airport. Oh, it was *lovely*! (*She returns to Hubback*) You want to see my pink form?

Hubback No fear!

Agatha You may as well see it now and get it over with.

Hubback I don't want to see it at *all*!

Agatha (*surprised*) You don't?

Hubback Not likely.

Agatha They said at the travel agents that we'd have to show it as soon as we got here.

Hubback (*realizing*) Oh, *that* pink form——

Agatha (*grinning*) You dirty old man ...! (*She laughs*)

Hubback (*flustered*) You don't have to show your pink form to *me*!

Agatha Oh, well—please yourself I'm sure. Anyhow—I've arrived! That's the main thing, isn't it?

Mrs Hubback (*without enthusiasm*) I suppose so——

Agatha My sister's seeing to the rest of the luggage. We got a taxi, you see. There was nobody from the travel agency to meet us at the airport like they said there would be. I can't understand it. (*She marches to the arch*) What's she doing out there? (*Calling loudly*) Fiona! What are you doing? Come on in here!

The Hubbacks cringe, their peaceful holiday in tatters

Agatha comes pounding back from the archway

She's slow, that's the trouble with my sister. Very slow. Doesn't know if it's Pancake Tuesday or Mafeking night. (*She advances on Hubback*) Now! Would you like to see my passport?

Hubback (*looking bewildered*) No, thanks. I've got one of my own.
Agatha But that's not the same as *mine*, is it?
Hubback Of course it isn't. Got a different picture in the front.
Agatha (*laughing delightedly*) Oh, you are a one!

Agatha pushes Hubback playfully, and he nearly drops the luggage

And they say foreigners have got no sense of humour! (*She marches up to the archway*)

Hubback and his wife exchange looks

Hubback Foreigners? What's she talking about?
Agatha (*calling*) Fiona! Just bring the luggage inside! You don't have to unpack it out there! You're not going to sleep in the hall, you know! (*She returns downstage, a big smile on her face*) Don't misunderstand, mind. She's a nice woman, my sister. In her own way. It's just that she hasn't enjoyed the journey very much. She didn't want to come out here in the first place. You see, she hasn't got any spirit of adventure, that's her trouble. (*To Mrs Hubback*) Not like you and me, eh? I like adventure — and fun! Don't you, dear?

Mrs Hubback looks appalled. Hubback attempts to explain the misunderstanding

Hubback Look — I think there's something you should . . .
Agatha Of course there is! I am silly. I haven't told you my name, have I? Hepworth. Agatha Hepworth. British subject. (*She brandishes her passport*) You'll find it all in here. (*To Mrs Hubback*) Even my age!
Hubback I — I don't think you quite——
Agatha Oh, I'm so sorry!
Hubback What?
Agatha I forgot! (*To Mrs Hubback*) I clean forgot I was in a foreign country. Well, you do, don't you? This air travel's all so fast, isn't it? Know what I mean? (*To Hubback*) I don't suppose you speak much English, do you?
Hubback Well, I . . .
Agatha Silly of me not to realize right away. Never mind. I've got my Italian phrase book with me so we'll be all right.
Hubback I don't speak Italian!

Agatha stares at Hubback in horrified disbelief

Agatha Don't tell me I've chosen the only hotel in Italy that's got a manager who doesn't speak Italian?
Hubback (*desperately*) I'm *not*!
Agatha Not Italian?
Hubback Not the manager!

Agatha thinks for a moment

Agatha Then why are you holding my luggage?

Hubback Because you gave it to me!

Agatha You mean you're nothing to do with this hotel?

Hubback No! I'm just staying here, that's all.

Agatha (*laughing at her own stupidity*) Ooooh! You're on holiday? I'm ever so sorry. How could I do a thing like that? Do forgive me. How dreadful! Here—you'd better give those back to me, then. (*She tries to take her luggage from him*)

Hubback No, no. Never mind. It's all right. I'm quite used to them now. I'll put them down over here. (*He puts her things down* UR *and returns to her*)

Agatha Oh, thank you. That is kind. Fancy me thinking you were the manager. You must think I'm *awful*!

Hubback does not deny it

What's your name, then, dear?

Hubback Hubback. Brigadier Hubback.

Agatha An *Army* brigadier? I'd never have guessed.

Hubback (*defensively*) Why not?

Agatha Well, you haven't got your uniform on, have you? (*She laughs*)

Hubback I'm ex.

Agatha Oh, I see. You're past it now. Well, never mind, dear. Nice to meet you. (*She shakes his hand vigorously*)

Hubback How do you do. And that's my wife over there.

Agatha Oh, I *am* sorry——

Hubback (*quietly*) Yes. Too late to do anything about it now, though.

Agatha No, no—I meant—I'm sorry about me taking you for the manager. After all, you don't *look* Italian, do you? (*She peers at his face, closely*) Here—wait a minute . . .

Hubback What's the matter?

Agatha There's something familiar about your face. We haven't met before, have we?

Hubback Good God, no! I think I'd have remembered that.

Marisa comes in through the archway with a tray of tea. She has now changed into a pretty dress

Marisa I have brought your tea.

Marisa moves towards Mrs Hubback, but Agatha thinks the tea is for her

Agatha Oh, that *is* kind, dear! Just what I need. (*She takes the tray and puts it down on the table* DR. *She sits down, takes the lid off the pot and gives the tea a brisk stir*)

Marisa looks helplessly at Mrs Hubback who suffers as Agatha pours herself a cup of tea

Mrs Hubback *I* should like some tea.

Agatha Yes, I should, if I were you, dear. It looks very nice.

Marisa I will get some more. (*She starts towards the hall*)

Fiona Francis enters slowly through the archway. She is a few years younger than her sister, and has come on holiday very much against her will. She is laden down like a pack-mule with two suitcases, a small grip, a carrier bag, a brown paper parcel, her handbag and an umbrella. She comes in looking about apprehensively

The Hubbacks and Marisa watch her as she comes in. Agatha is busy with her tea

Agatha What took you so long?
Fiona I was collecting the cases. (*Pointedly*) *And* paying the taxi.
Agatha Don't worry. I'll pay *my* share.
Fiona What shall I do with them?
Agatha Well, I should put them down somewhere. (*She concentrates on her tea*)

Hubback and Marisa go to help Fiona with the luggage

Hubback (*politely*) Here—let *me* help you.

Fiona looks at Hubback suspiciously

Fiona Why? Are you the manager?
Hubback (*losing his temper a little*) No, I'm not the manager! I'm just a man helping you with your cases!
Fiona (*looking at Marisa*) What about *her*?
Hubback She's not the manager, either. I'm just staying here, and she's just swimming here.
Fiona *Swimming* here?
Hubback Er—working here! Oh, give me your cases!

Hubback and Marisa take Fiona's things and put them down with Agatha's. Fiona looks about the lounge unimpressed

Fiona I don't much like the look of this.
Agatha (*busy with her tea*) No, I didn't think you would.
Fiona It's not a bit like the picture in the brotcher.
Agatha Oh, yes, it is.
Fiona Oh, no, it isn't! The walls were green. I remember distinctly. (*Piously*) That's cheating, if you ask me.
Agatha There's no law against them putting on a coat of paint, is there?
Fiona I liked the walls green. Better than this colour.
Agatha Oh, blimey . . .! I should sit down if I were you.
Fiona Yes, I will. I'm quite exhausted. (*She sits down near Agatha, sees the tea that her sister is enjoying and looks a little put out*) You got yourself a cup of tea, then?
Agatha You can have one as well. You don't have to get your knickers in a twist.
Marisa I will get another cup.

Marisa exits through the archway

Hubback moves downstage, watching her go

Agatha This is my sister, Fiona Francis. (*To Fiona*) That's Colonel Hubback——

Hubback Brigadier, actually.
Agatha Yes, of course—Brigadier. And the one over there is his wife.
Hubback
Mrs Hubback } (*together*) { How do you do.
Fiona (*nervously*) Are we the only people staying here?
Agatha (*with a pained look*) Of course we're not the only people staying here!
Hubback Good lord, no. They're packed in like sardines. And let me give you a word of warning. Dinner's at seven-thirty, so be on parade early or you'll be trampled in the rush! (*He chuckles*)
Fiona (*fearfully*) Oh, dear. I don't think I like the sound of that . . .
Agatha No, I didn't think you would!

Marisa returns with a cup and saucer

Thank you, dear. (*She pours a cup of tea for Fiona and adds milk*) There you are. A nice cup of tea. At least you can't complain about that.
Fiona (*pessimistically*) I haven't tasted it yet, have I?
Agatha Well, it's Tetley's Tea Bags, same as you get at home, so get on with it!

Fiona takes a sip, then exclaims

Fiona Here—they've made it with water!
Agatha What do *you* make it with? Castor oil?
Fiona We're not supposed to drink the water. That's what they told us at the travel agents.
Agatha (*patiently*) The water's been boiled, hasn't it? So any foreign bodies floating about in it'll be dead by now, won't they?
Fiona Foreign bodies?
Agatha Yes—tadpoles—sharks—things like that. Oh, get on with it!

Fiona eyes the tea suspiciously. Mrs Hubback looks on with the air of a martyr

Mrs Hubback *I* should like a cup of tea.
Marisa Oh, yes—of course! I will order another pot for you. (*To Agatha*) Please do you have your pink form from the travel agency?
Agatha Ah! there you are, you see, Captain! I knew someone would want to see my pink form sooner or later. (*She takes the pink form from her handbag and gives it to Marisa*) There you are, dear.
Marisa Grazie.
Agatha Definitely.

Marisa exits through the archway, pinching Hubback's bottom as she passes behind him

Hubback calls out as before. Agatha is startled and looks at Hubback in surprise. Hubback assumes an air of innocence

Agatha You all right, dear?
Mrs Hubback (*wearily*) Don't worry, Mrs Hepworth. It's only the hot sun shining on my husband's neck. It makes him cry out, occasionally.

Agatha Oh, dear. . . . An old war wound, I suppose?

Hubback Yes, you could say that! (*He catches his wife's eye—and hastily moves away*)

Fiona (*unwrapping a pill from inside a tissue*) Do you think I ought to take this pill now?

Agatha You were supposed to take that before you left. It's for travel sickness!

Fiona I never thought.

Agatha That's nothing new. (*She sips her tea*)

Hubback is drifting towards the archway, hoping to escape

You going somewhere, Colonel?

Hubback stops

Hubback Er—Brigadier.

Agatha What?

Hubback Brigadier. Not—er——

Agatha Oh, yes, of course! I am sorry. I keep calling you the wrong thing, don't I?

Hubback Yes, you do.

Agatha I shall have to try not to.

Hubback Yes, you will! (*He wanders behind the sofa, exchanging a look with his wife*)

Agatha sighs contentedly, and looks at Fiona with a smile

Agatha Well . . . we *got* here, eh, Fiona?

Fiona I'm surprised I'm still in one piece.

Agatha sighs, gets up and moves over to Hubback

Agatha (*quietly*) She's done nothing but grumble all the way here.

Fiona It's not natural going up in the air. I told you we should have gone by train.

Agatha Don't be daft. Would have taken longer by train, wouldn't it?

Fiona Couldn't have taken *much* longer! We were stuck at the airport for five hours before we even got on a plane. And when we *did* set off I thought the pilot would never stop driving along that runway. I began to think he must have decided to go by road after all!

Agatha Well, if you'd spoken nicely to him he might have let *you* drive. (*She winks at Hubback*)

Fiona It's not safe up in the air . . .

Agatha You're the one who's not safe. You ought to be kept in a cage.

Mrs Hubback makes an effort, and addresses Agatha, politely

Mrs Hubback Mrs Hepworth—is your husband coming on later?

Agatha I hope not, dear. He's dead!

Mrs Hubback Oh. I am sorry.

Agatha No need to be. He was a mean old skinflint was my Harold. If he could get out of spending his money he would. And did. As a result, when he died he left a sackful. And he left it all to me. Best day's work he ever did. (*She chuckles, happily*) If he knew how I was spending his money he'd turn in his grave!

Fiona He was cremated ...

Agatha (*giving Fiona a look before continuing*) So that's why me and Fiona's come out here.

Fiona *I* didn't want to come out here. What's wrong with Eastcliffe, that's what I want to know.

Agatha I'll tell you what's wrong with Eastcliffe! It's common! That's what it is. Common. Same old faces year after year. You don't meet *class* at Eastcliffe. Not like the Captain and his wife

Hubback (*warning*) Ah ...!

Hubback } (*together*) { Brigadier!
Agatha

Fiona I knew a woman went abroad once. She was bitten by a bug. They brought her back in a box.

Agatha (*to Mrs Hubback*) She's a little ray of sunshine, isn't she?

Hubback Oh, you don't have to worry, Miss Francis. You'll be all right here. Once you get used to it.

Fiona (*alarmed*) What have I got to get used to?

Agatha *Now* you've got her going——

Hubback Well ... er ... things are ... different here, one has to admit.

Fiona Different?

Hubback Well, you didn't come all the way out here to eat fish and chips, now did you?

Fiona Why not? I like fish and chips.

Hubback Yes, I thought you would ...! Well ... er ... the food here is a *bit* different.

Fiona I'm not eating none of them octopuses!

Agatha You don't get octopuses here! Can't you even read the brotcher? Octopuses is Spain!

Fiona (*miserably*) I bet you can't tell *what* you're eating half the time. If they eat frogs' legs in France, heaven knows what we'll get here!

Agatha You're not going to get anything like that.

Fiona How can I be sure? I bet you they'll disguise it.

Agatha Well, if they disguise it, you won't know, will you?

Fiona *I* may not know, but my stomach soon will!

Agatha After twenty years of your shepherd's pie I reckon your stomach's ready for anything.

Fiona I bet I'll get Spanish tummy——

Agatha (*crossing to Fiona*) How can you get Spanish tummy? You're in Italy!

Mrs Hubback And in Italy they do tend to eat rather a lot of pasta.

Fiona I'm not having none of them!

Agatha (*patiently*) Fiona ... pasta isn't plural.

Mrs Hubback I have one golden rule whenever I travel abroad. When in doubt—order an omelette. And never—*ever*—be without your pills.

Fiona (*alarmed*) *Pills*? What do I want pills for? You mean I'm going to be ill?

Agatha Oh, you've really got her going now. (*To Fiona*) Finish your tea. You'll be all right.

Fiona I don't want no more tea.

Mrs Hubback You're lucky to have had *any* . . .

Agatha Oh, dear me! You still haven't had your tea, have you?

Mrs Hubback No. Marisa seems to have forgotten all about it.

Hubback I'll go and find her, shall I? Chase her up a bit!

Mrs Hubback (*giving him an icy look*) I think you've done enough chasing for one day.

Agatha (*to Mrs Hubback*) Seems a very nice hotel, Mrs Hubback dear, from what I've seen of it so far. Classy—you know what I mean? And very friendly. I'm all for that. A nice, friendly atmosphere where we can all be one big happy family! You know, like a sort of a holiday camp! I bet *you* like that sort of thing the same as I do?

Mrs Hubback (*horrified*) No! I prefer peace and quiet.

Agatha (*staring in disbelief*) Peace and quiet? No!

Mrs Hubback (*firmly*) Peace and quiet—yes!

Agatha (*sitting on the sofa beside Mrs Hubback*) Oh, I expect you're shy, is that it? A bit shy? Well, a lot of people are at first. But don't you worry, dear. You stick to me. I'll look after you.

Mrs Hubback Well, actually, Mrs Hepworth—we are supposed to be going home tomorrow, so——

Agatha We'll have to move quickly, then, won't we? Look—I tell you what—as soon as we've unpacked we'll all go down to the beach, eh? (*She smiles enthusiastically*) We'll round up a few of the others from the hotel—and then we can organize some games! Like *It's A Knockout* on the telly. How about that, eh?

The Hubbacks look appalled by the prospect

Mrs Hubback Well, I . . . I really think the people staying here do rather prefer to keep themselves to themselves. Don't they, Charles?

Hubback Yes, they certainly do!

Agatha (*undeterred*) I expect they want jollying-up a bit. Just needs someone to break the ice. And I'm very good as an ice-breaker! (*She laughs happily*)

Fiona I want to go to my room . . .

Agatha (*rising and crossing to Fiona*) All right, love—we'll go and unpack. And then—everybody down to the beach!

Fiona I don't want to go down to the beach.

Agatha I beg your pardon?

Fiona I want to go to my room and have a lie down. (*She gets up to go*)

Agatha You didn't come all this way to have a lie down! Go and look at the view! (*She gives Fiona a push*)

Fiona goes, disconsolately, out onto the patio and wanders away out of sight

(*To the Hubbacks*) I'll just go and find the manager. Get someone to see to our bags. Oh, Mrs Hubback dear, we're going to have such fun!

Agatha sails out through the archway

Hubback Oh, my God ...! (*He crosses, unhappily, to* L *of the sofa*)
Mrs Hubback Beach games indeed! I knew something like this would happen. I knew we should have taken a villa in Corfu like we did last year.
Hubback I suppose we can always keep away from the main beach. Go up the other end.
Mrs Hubback (*looking at her husband, witheringly*) Charles, that is where the nudists go.
Hubback Well, she'd never recognize us there!
Mrs Hubback That woman would recognize us *any*where! She's probably equipped with radar. Wherever we go from now on she'll creep up on us, beaming all over her face.
Hubback We can always escape.
Mrs Hubback Escape? It'll be like trying to get out of Colditz. If our plane doesn't take off we may be trapped here for days! Charles—something will have to be done.

Agatha returns from the hall. She moves to C

Agatha I can't find anybody out there. They all seem to have disappeared.
Hubback (*quietly*) I expect they heard you coming.
Agatha What did you say?
Hubback I said I expect they'll soon be coming.
Agatha I hope so. (*Enthusiastically*) I want to get unpacked and out. (*To Mrs Hubback*) Sorry to keep you hanging about, dear.
Mrs Hubback Well ... as a matter of fact, we ... we do have to do something.
Agatha (*ominously*) *Do* something?
Mrs Hubback Yes. Er—do something. (*She passes the buck*) Don't we, Charles?
Hubback What? Ah. Yes. Yes, we do! We have to ... er ... do something. Something fairly important. And we have to go and ... and do it.
Agatha (*to Mrs Hubback*) Now?
Mrs Hubback Yes, now. Come along, Charles! (*She gets up*)

The Hubbacks move quickly towards the stairs. Agatha goes after them

Agatha Are you going to be long?

The Hubbacks stop

Hubback Er——(*He looks at his wife*)
Mrs Hubback Yes.
Hubback (*to Agatha*) Yes.
Agatha *How* long?
Hubback Er——(*He looks at his wife again*)
Mrs Hubback Long enough.
Hubback (*to Agatha*) Long enough.

Agatha Long enough for what?

Hubback Er——(*He looks at his wife yet again*)

Mrs Hubback Long enough for her to unpack!

Hubback Ah—yes! (*He turns to Agatha*) Long enough for you to unpack.

Agatha Oh, I see!

Hubback Do you? Oh, splendid. That's settled, then.

Agatha So by the time we've unpacked——

Mrs Hubback (*quietly*) *We*'ll have disappeared . . .

Hubback (*to Agatha*) *We*'ll have disappeared! (*He corrects himself quickly*) I mean—we'll have finished whatever it is we're doing and we'll be back.

Agatha Righto, then. You'd better go and do it.

Hubback (*gratefully*) Yes—rather! Come on, darling! We'll go and . . . and do it. (*He drags Mrs Hubback towards the stairs*)

Agatha (*firmly*) And we'll meet you back here in five minutes! All right?

The Hubbacks react and disappear quickly upstairs. Fiona reappears outside, looking down at the view

Agatha turns and sees Fiona

Not thinking of jumping over, are you?

Fiona turns. She is now wearing sun-glasses

Oh, my God! I thought it was the Mafia.

Fiona Well, as I'd bought them I thought I may as well put them on.

Agatha Yes. Good idea. All you need now is a white stick and a dog.

Marisa comes in from the hall with a tray of tea for one

Marisa Oh! Mrs Hubback has gone?

Agatha Yes. They've gone upstairs to "do something".

Marisa But I have brought her tea.

Agatha I don't think she wants any tea now. Never mind, dear. Put it down there. *I'll* have it. I could do with another cup.

Marisa But I have charged it to her room.

Agatha (*smiling, logically*) Well, she ordered it, didn't she? (*Turning to Fiona*) There you are, you see, Fiona. Isn't that a lovely view?

Agatha joins Fiona and they both look out to sea. Marisa puts the tray on the table DLC

Julian Whittle comes down the stairs, briskly. He is a bright young man with an eye for the girls. He carries a clipboard and wears his official name tag on his blazer

Seeing the shapely Marisa bending over the tray, Julian smiles appreciatively. Unaware of Agatha and Fiona, he creeps up and is about to put his arms around her. Marisa does not even have to look round to know who it is

Marisa Not now, Mr Whittle!

Julian (*looking aggrieved*) How did you know it was me?

Marisa Because you *always* do that. You are supposed to be working!

Julian No, I'm not. I *was* meeting two old bags off Flight four-one-three but they've been delayed.

Agatha and Fiona turn in unison and look at him

Agatha Oh, no, they haven't!

Julian turns and sees Agatha and Fiona watching him grimly

Julian Oh, God!

Agatha No, but you're getting warm. (*She goes to Julian*) Perhaps we'd better introduce ourselves. I am Mrs Hepworth and the other old bag is my sister, Fiona.

Julian But I ... I thought your plane was delayed.

Agatha It was.

Fiona (*joining Agatha*) Yes. Five hours at London Airport sitting on my backside ...

Agatha (*giving Fiona a weary look*) Fiona ... we don't want to hear about your backside.

Marisa giggles

Julian I thought it was a *seven* hour delay.

Agatha Must have had a strong tail-wind, then, mustn't we?

Julian (*ingratiatingly*) If I'd known I'd have been at the airport to meet you. With a car! (*He smiles, desperate to regain lost ground*)

Fiona (*quite moved*) Oh. ... That's very kind of you, young man. Very kind indeed. Isn't that kind, Agatha?

Agatha Kind? He's only doing his job. Or rather—*not* doing his job! (*To Julian*) I presume you *are* our tour representative?

Julian smiles, sycophantically

Julian Yes, that's right. I'm Whittle from Warwick.

Agatha You were behaving more like Charlie from Chester!

Julian (*aside to Marisa*) Why didn't you tell me they were here?

Marisa I tried to, but you had your mind on other things.

Marisa giggles and exits into the hall

Julian watches Marisa go

Fiona (*wandering, thoughtfully, across to the sofa*) I don't understand. They said at the travel agent that our tour representative was called Julian ... (*She sits, confused*)

Julian Yes! That's me! Julian Whittle.

Fiona Oh. ... The company only used your *first* name.

Julian Yes. They think it lends a happy, friendly atmosphere to the proceedings.

Agatha You haven't started off very well, then, have you, Mr Whittle?

Fiona "Julian", Agatha.

Agatha He's still Mr Whittle to an old bag like me!

Julian starts to go after Marisa

Now where are you off to?

Julian I'm just going to do those things that I have left undone.

Julian goes, quickly, into the hall

Agatha (*going to pour herself a cup of tea from the new pot*) He doesn't seem to have his mind on the job.

The Hubbacks come creeping down the stairs and head for the glass doors in the hope of escaping unseen, but Agatha has eyes in the back of her head

And where are you two creeping off to?

The Hubbacks stop nervously

Hubback W-what?

Agatha You didn't take very long. Whatever it was you had to do you did it very quickly. (*Suspiciously*) You weren't on your way to the beach, were you?

Hubback (*overdoing it*) The beach? Good lord, no! Never!

Agatha Because we arranged to meet in here. (*She smiles broadly*) Had you forgotten?

Hubback looks suitably surprised

Hubback Ah! It was in *here*, was it? We weren't quite sure.

Agatha Lucky I saw you, then, wasn't it?

Hubback Yes. We might have got away.

Agatha What?

Hubback Might have gone the wrong way!

Agatha Oh ... and then my sister and me might never have found you.

Hubback Yes. That *would* have been a shame, wouldn't it? (*He exchanges a look with his wife*)

Agatha (*suddenly realizing*) Oh, look, Mrs Hubback dear—I'm drinking your tea!

Mrs Hubback It's quite all right. I'm getting used to it now.

Agatha Well, I won't be long, dear. We'll soon be off to the beach. (*She finishes off her tea, hastily*)

Mrs Hubback Ah—well ... er ... I—I *was* thinking of ... of going to the village.

Agatha (*appalled*) The village? We can go to the village tonight. After dinner. I expect you know a few night spots—eh, General? (*She laughs, saucily*)

Mrs Hubback (*firmly*) *I* prefer to go to the village *now*!

Agatha (*looking at Mrs Hubback in surprise*) Oh, all right, then, dear. We'll *all* go.

Mrs Hubback What?!

Agatha We can save the beach games till tomorrow. (*She puts her cup down on the tray*) Come along, Fiona! Off we go!

Fiona I'd sooner go to my room and unpack.

Agatha You'll have plenty of time for that later on. (*To the others*) We've just got to go and sign the register and leave our passports at the desk and then we'll be ready. Come on, Fiona! Don't hang about.

Fiona (*gloomily, as they start to move*) All this foreign travel's over-rated. . . .

Agatha You haven't tried it yet. You never know your luck. You might meet Mr Right sitting down there on the piazza.

Fiona Who's Mr Right?

Agatha Your dream man, of course!

Fiona Well, if he's anything like your Harold it won't half be a nightmare.

Fiona and Agatha exit into the hall

The Hubbacks seize their opportunity and start to go quickly towards the patio

Julian returns and sees the Hubbacks

Julian (*reacting in alarm*) What the hell are *you* doing here?

Hubback (*astonished*) I *beg* your pardon, Whittle?

Julian (*desperately*) You're not supposed to *be* here!

Hubback Where?

Julian In this hotel!

Hubback Don't be daft. We're staying here.

Julian Not any more. You've gone.

Hubback Gone where?

Julian Gone home!

Hubback How can we have gone home when we're still here? You're losing your bottle, Whittle.

Mrs Hubback (*patiently*) The flights have been delayed. *You* know that. Instead of leaving today we're leaving tomorrow morning.

Julian No! Not tomorrow morning— *this* morning!

Hubback What are you talking about?

Julian Didn't you get my message?

Hubback What message?

Julian I left you a message out there at the desk last night. They rearranged the flights. Your plane went this morning!

The Hubbacks look shattered

Mrs Hubback But . . . but we're still here.

Hubback Oh, my God . . !

Mrs Hubback (*doomed*) I knew it! We're going to be trapped here with that dreadful woman for ever——

Hubback It's all *your* fault, Whittle.

Julian Yes, I thought it would be!

Hubback You told us that our plane was delayed until tomorrow.

Julian (*losing his temper*) That was before my message!

Hubback But I never *got* your message!

Julian Well, you *should* have done! (*Pacing away, wildly*) I wrote you a message—I left you a message—at least you could have *read* the bloody message!

The Hubbacks look at him, astonished at his outburst

Hubback Whittle . . . .!

Julian I'm—I'm sorry. I'm under a bit of a strain. (*He sits, abruptly, on the sofa* DL)

Mrs Hubback *You're* under a strain! What about us? Come along, Charles. I think we'll go back to our room.

Hubback Right!

The Hubbacks make for the stairs. Julian leaps up and races to intercept them

Julian No, you can't!

Hubback Why not?

Julian (*nervously*) Well—that's the *other* problem.

Mrs Hubback What other problem?

Julian You haven't *got* a room!

Hubback I beg your pardon?

Julian You should have gone home! And the room that was *your* room is now *their* room!

Hubback Whose room?

Julian (*wildly*) Mrs Hepworth and her sister!

Hubback Oh, my God . . . !

Mrs Hubback But *we* haven't moved out yet.

Julian Exactly! That's the problem. You've got to move out before they can move in! (*He breaks away, distractedly, towards the glass doors*)

Mrs Hubback (*severely*) I have no intention of moving out.

Julian (*turning and looking at Mrs Hubback nervously*) What?

Mrs Hubback I intend to stay put.

Julian (*fearfully*) Y-y-you wouldn't do that?

Mrs Hubback I certainly would.

Julian You wouldn't!

Mrs Hubback I would.

Hubback (*to Julian*) She would.

Julian Well, you try telling Mrs Hepworth that!

Mrs Hubback No, Mr Whittle. *You* try telling Mrs Hepworth that.

Agatha and Fiona return from the hall. Agatha is carrying an envelope

Agatha (*breezing in cheerfully*) Righto, then—here we are! Didn't keep you waiting long, did we! (*She goes to Hubback*) Oh, Colonel—there was a message for you at the desk. (*She hands him the envelope*)

Hubback Oh. Thanks. (*He takes the envelope and glances at Julian*)

Julian cowers, apprehensively

Agatha Well, go on! Aren't you going to open it? You might have come up on the pools.

Hubback I don't think I have, somehow . . .

Agatha Well, open it and see what it says.

Hubback I *know* what it says. Don't I, Whittle?

Julian wishes he was a million miles away

Agatha Right! Off we go, then! (*She takes Mrs Hubback cosily by the arm*)

Oh, I'm really looking forward to seeing the village, Mrs Hubback dear.
Tell you what—I'll look after you, and you look after me! All right?

Mrs Hubback hastily feels ill and cries out loudly

Mrs Hubback Aah!!

They all look at her in surprise

Agatha Whatever's the matter?
Hubback Are you all right, darling?
Mrs Hubback I've suddenly got a headache. So—if you don't mind, Mrs
   Hepworth—I won't go into the village. Not just now.
Agatha Oh, dear. What a pity.
Hubback Yes. What a shame ...
Mrs Hubback I think I'll just go to my room and have a lie down.

Julian looks alarmed

Fiona That's what *I* wanted to do. ... (*She sits, disconsolately, on the sofa*)
Agatha (*to Fiona, sharply*) You can do it later! (*Then gently, to Mrs
   Hubback*) That's all right, dear. You go and have a nice lie down.
Mrs Hubback Thank you. (*She starts towards the stairs with a suitably heavy
   tread*)
Agatha And if I were you I'd lock your door.
Mrs Hubback Yes. I think I *will* ...!
Agatha I mean, you don't want to be disturbed, now do you?
Mrs Hubback No—certainly not!
Hubback (*joining his wife, eagerly*) Perhaps I'd better come with you,
   darling?
Agatha She said she didn't want to be disturbed.
Mrs Hubback It's quite all right, Mrs Hepworth. Charles *never* disturbs me.

   Mrs Hubback exits upstairs

Hubback (*quietly, as he goes*) I wouldn't dare ...!

   He disappears after his wife

Agatha quickly regains her high spirits, goes to Fiona and pulls her to her feet

Agatha Come on, then, Fiona! Mrs Hubback's headache doesn't have to
   stop *us* from going, does it?
Fiona What about *my* headache?
Agatha You haven't got a headache! Come on. You and me'll explore the
   village on our own.
Fiona (*grumbling*) It won't be like looking at the shops in Eastcliffe ...
Agatha Well, you can't expect to find your Boots and your Marks and
   Spencers, now can you?
Fiona That's what I'm worried about ...
Agatha (*buoyantly*) But they'll have something similar! Come on! (*She
   starts to propel Fiona towards the archway, then pauses to look back at the
   unhappy Julian*) Oh, and Mr Whittle——
Julian (*apprehensively*) Yes, Mrs Hepworth?

Agatha (*happily*) While we're down in the village, you can have our cases taken up to our room!

Agatha and Fiona exit into the hall

Julian sinks despondently onto the luggage

Black-out

The CURTAIN *falls*

SCENE 2

The same. Early that evening

The cases are still there but the tea-trays have been cleared away

As the CURTAIN rises Marisa is tidying the magazines on the table DR.

Julian comes marching in from the hall in a high state of anxiety

Julian *Now* what the hell am I supposed to do? There isn't an empty room anywhere in the town.

Marisa But the room *here* is for Mrs Hepworth and her sister. So the Brigadier and his wife will just have to go.

Julian (*wildly*) But they can't go! There isn't an aeroplane. What do you expect them to do? Walk on the water? He may be a brigadier but he can't do that.

Marisa Have you spoken to the manager?

Julian Spoken to him? I can't even find him! He's never here when there's a crisis. Where the hell does he hide himself all day?

Marisa (*going to Julian*) You must not get so excited. You must try to relax.

Julian How do you expect me to relax?

Marisa Well, why don't you put your arms around me? (*She smiles, invitingly*)

Julian looks at Marisa, surprised by this unexpected but delightful invitation

Julian What?

Marisa Put your arms around me.

Julian Oh. Right. (*He does so, but without much enthusiasm. He gives up and breaks way from her miserably*) It's no good. I can't concentrate! This is just my luck, isn't it?

Marisa (*innocently*) What is?

Julian Well, you're not usually co-operative like this! Why are you only co-operative when I'm in the middle of a crisis?

Marisa giggles

Agatha (*off*) Oh, Fiona! Do come *on*! Stop dawdling about!

Julian Oh, my God! She's here! (*He starts to go*)

Marisa Where are you going?

Julian I don't know, but I'm not staying here!

Marisa (*following Julian*) You will have to tell her about the room *some* time!

Julian and Marisa exit quickly through the glass doors

Agatha pounds in from the hall. She has bought a few things in the village and is wearing a bright sun-hat

Fiona follows Agatha in, not having enjoyed her walk at all. She is carrying a large paper carrier bag

Fiona Oh, my feet . . . ! I can't think why we had to go down to the village in the first place. (*She sits wearily on the sofa* DL)
Agatha You're supposed to soak up the atmosphere. How can you go back home and tell your neighbours about foreign travel if you haven't soaked up the atmosphere?

Fiona takes off a shoe and massages her foot

Pause

Fiona There was a terrible smell.
Agatha Well, put your shoe back on!
Fiona No—going down to the village. Don't say you didn't notice?
Agatha Well, of course I noticed! It's part of the charm, isn't it?
Fiona Oh. (*Pause*) Is that what you meant by soaking up the atmosphere?
Agatha No, of course not!
Fiona Got trouble with their drains, if you ask me.
Agatha Can't you ever notice anything but drains? (*She starts to go*) Oh, well—come on. We may as well go and unpack now. (*She comes face to face with their suitcases and reacts angrily*) They're still here!
Fiona What?
Agatha They haven't even moved our cases yet. Just you wait till I find that Mr Whittle. Call himself an organizer. He couldn't organize a piss-up in a brewery.

Agatha sails out to the hall, calling as she goes

  Mr Whittle! Where are you? Mr Whittle . . . !

Fiona opens her carrier bag furtively, takes out a large floppy sun-hat. She puts it on. It covers her face

Agatha returns

Agatha I can't understand this hotel. It's like a ghost town. (*She sees Fiona in her hat*) Oh, my God . . . ! There's no sign of anybody out there. No manager. Nobody at the desk. And no sign of Mr Whittle! Oh, well, never mind, eh? We can get on with these while we're waiting. (*She produces some picture postcards from her bag*)
Fiona What are they?
Agatha The picture postcards I bought in the village. You got your pen?
Fiona Yes, but . . .
Agatha Right—let's get on with them, then! (*She sits at the table* DR)

Fiona abandons her sun-hat and goes, reluctantly, to sit at the table with Agatha

Fiona I don't see why we have to write postcards *now*——
Agatha (*logically*) Well, we're *here*, aren't we?
Fiona Yes, but . . .
Agatha Right! *Tell* them we're here! (*She thrusts some of the postcards at Fiona*)
Fiona Couldn't we do them tomorrow?
Agatha You'll forget them tomorrow. You'll be so busy having a nice time you'll forget all about them. Do it now, then they're out of the way. Leave you to think about nothing but pleasure. You know what *you're* like about pleasure. Well, you'll be able to *think* about it.
Fiona Oh, all right . . . (*She considers them, bleakly*)

Pause

Agatha begins to write

Fiona (*pondering*) I don't know what to put.
Agatha Tell 'em you're enjoying yourself.
Fiona But I'm not.
Agatha Well tell 'em you're *not* enjoying yourself, then!

Pause

Agatha and Fiona write

(*Looking at Fiona*) Who's that one to?
Fiona Mrs Wilkinson.
Agatha What have you put?
Fiona (*reading*) "Mrs Wilkinson, Twenty-two Ferndale Avenue——"
Agatha Not that side—the other side! What have you put on the other side?

Fiona turns the cards over and looks at it

Fiona The picture's on the other side.
Agatha The other side of the back!
Fiona Oh. (*She turns the card over again*) Oh, I haven't put anything there yet. (*She considers for a moment*) Shall I tell her about the drains?
Agatha No, Fiona. She doesn't want to know about the drains.
Fiona She would if she was thinking of coming here.
Agatha Well, she's not, is she?
Fiona How do *you* know? She might be thumbing through the brotcher at this moment.
Agatha (*patiently*) Look—just put "This is a beautiful place. Wish you were with us."
Fiona But I don't.
Agatha That doesn't matter! She's not likely to catch the next plane.
Fiona (*looking at the picture on the other side*) But this isn't *here*. This is San Remo.
Agatha What of it?
Fiona But I haven't been there.

Agatha You've got two weeks. There's plenty of time.

Pause

Fiona But if I haven't been there, how do I know it's a beautiful place?

Agatha It doesn't matter whether you've been there or not! She's not going to check up, is she?

Fiona (*piously*) Oh, I couldn't do that. That would be lying. (*She starts to write, resting the card on a magazine*)

> *Marisa enters through the glass doors, carrying some flowers*

Agatha looks up

Agatha Oh, hallo, dear. Glad *some*one's about.

Marisa (*crossing to them*) You are writing postcards already? (*She goes to arrange the flowers in a vase*)

Agatha Oh, yes. I like to get them off early, then they're out of the way. How are you getting on, Fiona?

Fiona (*writing, laboriously*) All right . . .

Agatha You're not writing "War and Peace", you know. (*Thoughtfully*) I think I'll send one to Mrs Fenwick . . .

Fiona (*without looking up*) You don't like Mrs Fenwick.

Agatha No, I know. But I want to pay her back for the one she sent me from the South of France. (*She shows the card to Marisa*) What do you think of that one, dear?

Marisa Beautiful.

Agatha (*grinning with relish*) Yes! That'll show her! Fiona—haven't you finished that one yet?

Fiona Almost. (*She concludes by writing around the side of the address, and then sits back, satisfied with her efforts*)

Agatha Well? What have you put?

Fiona (*reading*) "We are three minutes from the gently sloping beach of honey-coloured sand . . ."

Agatha exchanges a look with Marisa

Agatha What?

Fiona ". . . and the warm caressing Mediterranean sea. Behind us the hillside villas gleam white and fresh amongst the pencil-like cypress trees and colour-drunk flowers."

Agatha The *what*?

Fiona (*looking up*) Colour-drunk flowers.

Agatha I see. Go on.

Fiona (*reading again*) "The air is warm and heavy with scent and we are enjoying these enchanted shores." (*She looks up for approval*)

Agatha (*astonished*) How did you think all that up?

Fiona It's all here in the brotcher! (*She waves the brochure at Agatha*)

Agatha Well, I suppose it's better than telling her about the drains.

Fiona What have *you* put, then?

Agatha (*reading*) "Spending two weeks on the Italian Riveera. It's very nice and very expensive. I bet you wish you were here." There! That's to the point, isn't it?

Fiona Yes. I think she'll get the message.

Agatha I wonder where that Mr Whittle's hiding himself. . . . You'd better go and find him for me, Marisa dear.

Marisa Oh. Yes. Of course. I will try . . .

Marisa moves towards the hall

Hubback comes down the stairs and sees Marisa. He is dressed for dinner

Hubback Ah, Marisa! Just going swimming, eh?

Marisa giggles

Marisa No. I am going working.

Hubback Oh. Pity.

Marisa But *you* are not dressed for swimming.

Hubback No. I'm dressed for drinking. (*He chuckles*) Just had a bath. Clean shirt. All that sort of thing. (*Leering at her*) And now I'm at the ready!

Marisa For a gin and tonic.

Hubback (*disappointed*) Oh, all right. Please yourself.

Marisa exits into the hall, giving Hubback a friendly pinch on the bottom as she passes him

Hubback cries out in surprise and delight. Agatha and Fiona look at him. Hubback sees them and laughs, embarrassed

Agatha You weren't even standing in the sunshine that time, were you?

Hubback hastily changes the subject

Hubback You—you enjoyed the village?

Agatha Oh, yes. It's lovely. You liked it, didn't you, Fiona?

Fiona It was all right once we'd got past them drains.

Agatha Fiona!

Hubback Ah—the drains. Yes. Well, one has to admit—the drains are not good. That's something you have to say about the Italians. If you have to say anything about them at all. Their drains are not good. That's one thing you *can* say about we British—we're very strong on sewage.

Agatha Is your wife all right now, Brigadier?

Hubback (*without thinking*) Yes—fine! Just having a stroll in the garden.

Fiona Oh, she's better, then?

Hubback (*blankly*) Better than what?

Fiona She had a headache! Don't you remember?

Hubback (*remembering*) Ah! Yes. Of course. So she did. Well, I—

Agatha She *must* be feeling better if she's gone for a walk. (*She puts away her postcards and pen*)

Hubback Ah—well—no—she's not exactly *better* . . .

Fiona You said she was fine.

Hubback Yes. I did, didn't I? That was stupid of me . . . Well, her

headache's better, but—er—now she's got toothache. Very bad tooth-
ache.
Agatha Is that why she went for a walk in the garden?
Hubback Ah—well—er—

Marisa enters from the hall with a gin and tonic

Marisa One gin and tonic.
Hubback Thank God for that! (*He takes it, gratefully, has a big sip and sits
on the sofa*)
Agatha (*to Marisa*) Did you find Mr Whittle, dear?
Marisa He is just coming. (*She goes to the archway to await Julian*)
Agatha About time, too! If we don't get up to our room and unpacked
soon, my frocks'll be all creased. Then I *shall* look a mess, shan't I?

Hubback looks unlikely to contradict her

Julian comes in, nervously, from the hall

Agatha Ah! there you are, Mr Whittle! We couldn't think where you'd got
to.
Julian I . . . I was just going for a walk.
Agatha You, as well? This is no time for walking!
Julian Isn't it? Oh, I thought it was.
Agatha You were wrong.
Julia Yes, I thought I would be . . . !

*Agatha rises, moves close to Julian and peers at him, fixedly. Julian shifts
apprehensively*

Agatha Now, Mr Whittle! Have you *done* all those things you ought to
have done?
Julian Er—yes. I *think* so.
Agatha No, you haven't!
Julian Haven't I?
Agatha Oh, no. They're still here.
Julian Sorry?
Agatha The bags.
Julian B-b-bags?
Agatha The bags up there!

Julian sees the suitcases and pretends to be surprised

Julian Good heavens! They're still down here!
Agatha Exactly. They are still down here when they should be up there.
They should be unpacked by now, Mr Whittle. There should be clothes
hanging up in wardrobes. Washing things in the bathroom. Dick Francis
novels by the bedside. By now, my sister and I should have bathed and
changed and be down here, smelling of duty-free toilet water, taking an
aperitif with the General prior to taking our places in the dining-room for
our first gastronomic delight in sunny Italy. But instead of that we're
sitting here like a couple of displaced persons because you have been too
bloody lazy to have our bags taken up to our room!

A long pause

Julian (*nervously*) Well ... you see ... there's a very good reason for that. Isn't there, Brigadier?

Hubback decides to escape before the bomb goes up. He finishes his drink hastily

Hubback I'd better go and find Audrey. (*He starts to go*)
Julian You don't have to do that! You don't have to go!
Hubback (*reasonably*) Well, I've finished my gin.

Julian clutches desperately onto Hubback's arm. Agatha is between them, watching in astonishment

Julian You usually have two or three before dinner!

Hubback and Julian struggle a little

Hubback Yes, I know I do, but——
Julian So you don't have to go! Not yet!
Hubback Yes, I do! (*He escapes from Julian's clutches*) Audrey may have fallen in the pool for all I know.
Julian Well, she can *swim*, can't she?
Hubback (*quietly*) Yes—unfortunately ...

Hubback disappears quickly into the garden

Marisa I think I am wanted in the bar. (*She collects Hubback's empty glass and starts to go*)
Julian (*in panic*) Don't *you* go, too!

Marisa just grins at him and runs out into the hall

Julian turns and finds Agatha fixing him with a beady eye. He cringes visibly

Agatha Well, Mr Whittle?
Julian (*miserably*) I feel as if I'm going in front of a firing squad.
Agatha You may be. There's plenty of time before dawn. (*Pause*) My sister and I are waiting.
Julian W-waiting?
Agatha For an explanation as to why our bags are still down here when they should be up there.
Julian Yes. Yes, I see. ... Er ... I wonder how I can put this ... ?
Fiona (*helpfully*) Perhaps there's a shortage of staff?
Julian Yes! Yes, of course! That's it! We're very short-staffed.

Agatha looks at Julian and smiles broadly

Agatha Well, why didn't you say so in the first place?
Julian Because I hadn't thought of it ...
Agatha If there's a shortage of staff, me and Fiona can give you a hand. We can manage a few bags between the three of us. Come on, Fiona—off we go! (*She moves towards their luggage*)

Fiona follows Agatha. Julian pursues them nervously

Julian Ah! No!

Agatha stops and turns

Agatha What?
Julian It's not just that.
Agatha Not just what?
Julian Shortage of staff.
Agatha Not just shortage of staff?
Julian No. Shortage of . . . of other things as well.
Agatha What other things?
Julian Important things.
Agatha How important?
Julian Very important.
Fiona They had a game like this on the telly once, everybody asking questions . . .
Agatha Well, if we're very patient perhaps Mr Whittle will give us some answers. (*To Julian*) Well? What else are we short of, Mr Whittle?
Julian Well . . . we're . . . we're actually rather short of . . . of a . . . (*He gestures, feebly*).
Fiona A ball?
Julian No. No—a . . . a— (*He gestures differently*)
Fiona A box?
Julian No, no! A . . . a—(*He gestures largely*)
Fiona Ah! A *room*?
Julian Yes!
Agatha (*ominously*) A *what*?
Julian A—a room. You know what a room is. Large—square—with a . . .
Agatha I know what a room is!
Julian Yes, I thought you would. . . .
Agatha (*erupting*) Are you trying to tell me that we haven't got a room?
Julian No!
Agatha We *have* got a room?
Julian Yes!
Agatha I'm finding it very hard to follow your conversation.
Julian Oh, good!
Fiona If we've got a room, why can't we go to it?
Agatha Thank you, Fiona. That's just what *I* was thinking.

They wait for Julian's explanation

Julian Well . . . how can I put this? I mean—I know exactly the sort of room you'd like.
Fiona (*pleased*) Oh, good! You see, Agatha? He knows what we like.
Julian (*enthusiastically*) Oh, yes! I can just visualize it. A nice big room. Furniture. Beds. Wardrobes. Tables. All that sort of thing. Bathroom. Lovely big bathroom. Towels. Soap. A nice, big, sunny, *un*occupied room.
Agatha (*laughing*) Well, of course it's got to be unoccupied! Wouldn't be any good having a room with people in it, would it? Really, Mr Whittle—

of course we want an *unoccupied* room! (*She is about to pick up a case*)
Julian Well, that isn't the sort of room we've got.

Agatha stops laughing, puts down the case and faces Julian

Agatha Are you trying to tell me that there are other people in our room?
Julian (*nodding, miserably*) Yes ...!
Fiona People in our room?
Julian I'm afraid so.
Agatha Mr Whittle! My sister and I have had a long journey. We were very late leaving London Airport ...
Fiona Five hours on my backside. ...
Agatha We've spent two hours walking around the village ...
Fiona Past all the drains ...
Agatha And now we're ready for a bath and a tidy-up before we have our dinner. Are you trying to tell me that we have been the victims of double-booking?
Julian Well, you see—they should have gone home this morning! They thought that their plane was delayed. But it wasn't, and they missed it.
Agatha If they missed their plane that's *their* hard luck.
Fiona Yes. All rooms are to be vacated by twelve o'clock. It says so in the brotcher.
Agatha You have read your own company's brotcher, I presume, Mr Whittle?
Julian Oh, yes! I've read it twice!
Fiona Then you must know that all rooms have to be vacated by twelve noon.
Julian (*desperately*) Yes, I know—but I can't get them out!
Agatha You leave it to me. I'll get 'em out all right! (*She strides, determinedly, to the archway and calls*) Marisa!

But it is Mrs Hubback who comes in from the hall at that moment, dressed for dinner

Ah! Hullo, Mrs Hubback dear! Had a nice walk?
Mrs Hubback Oh, just a stroll, Mrs Hepworth. Nothing too energetic. I think I left my book in here. (*She goes to get her book from the table* DR)
Agatha I'm glad your headache's better.
Mrs Hubback Is it?
Fiona Well, that's what your husband said.
Mrs Hubback Oh, did he? Yes, it's quite gone now!
Fiona (*frostily*) What about your *tooth*ache?
Mrs Hubback (*vaguely*) Toothache?
Fiona You had toothache!
Mrs Hubback Did I?
Fiona Well, that's what your husband said!
Mrs Hubback Oh, did he? Yes, of course—*that* toothache! Yes, I've got that. Very badly. It's just about—(*She is about to show where the pain is but hesitates, cautiously*) Did he say where it was?
Fiona No ...

Mrs Hubback (*relieved*) Ah—well, it's there! (*She opens her mouth and points inside, muttering indistinctly*) You see—right at the back there . . . that one there . . .

They all gather round and bend down to peer up into her gaping mouth

Agatha Oh, nasty . . ! By the way—I forgot—did you see your husband out in the garden?
Mrs Hubback No. I left Charles upstairs having a bath.
Fiona He's lucky to have a bath to have a bath *in*.
Agatha But he went outside to look for you.
Fiona Yes. He thought you might have fallen in the swimming pool.

Marisa comes in from the hall.

Marisa You called?
Agatha Ah, yes—Marisa dear, would you ask the manager to come and see me, please?
Julian (*nervously*) The manager?
Agatha I presume there *is* a manager in this hotel?
Julian Yes—but you can never find him!
Agatha I'm sure Marisa will be able to find him. Won't you, dear?
Marisa I will try.

Marisa exchanges an anxious look with Julian and exits into the hall

Agatha We have a bit of a problem, you see, Mrs Hubback.

Julian shrinks, visibly

Mrs Hubback Yes. I know. And I'm very sorry, of course. But I'm afraid there is absolutely no question of the Brigadier and me vacating *our* room.
Agatha (*realizing*) You don't mean it's *your* room that me and Fiona should be in?
Mrs Hubback You mean you didn't know?
Agatha No, I did *not*! (*She glares at Julian*)
Julian Well, I . . . I didn't get around to that bit.
Agatha No, I should think you didn't!
Mrs Hubback This is very embarrassing for us all, but I'm sure you realize, Mrs Hepworth, that until everything is sorted out there can be no question of you moving into *our* room. It just isn't possible.
Fiona (*grumbling*) I don't see why not . . .
Agatha Fiona—will you leave this to me!
Fiona All right, then—*you* tell her to get out of our room!
Agatha Fiona! Pull yourself together!
Fiona (*sulking*) Well, tell her . . .

Fiona and Julian wait for Vesuvius to erupt. But Agatha goes to Mrs Hubback with a big, wide, friendly smile

Agatha Of *course* I realize that, Mrs Hubback dear!

They all look astonished

Julian You do?

Mrs Hubback You do?

Agatha I wouldn't *dream* of turning you out of your room.

Mrs Hubback Wouldn't you?

Julian Wouldn't you?

Fiona *I* would!

Agatha We don't want to go and spoil your holiday, now do we?

Fiona What about *my* holiday?

Agatha (*snapping*) Your holiday hasn't started yet!

Fiona That's what I'm complaining about.

Agatha Fiona, how can you be so selfish? Poor Mrs Hubback. With her headache. And her toothache. And the Colonel with his war wound. You think I could turn them out? (*To Mrs Hubback*) You can have our room for as long as you want it, dear.

Mrs Hubback is astonished at such unexpected generosity

Mrs Hubback Well, that's very thoughtful of you, Mrs Hepworth. Very thoughtful indeed. I really must go and tell Charles. He *will* be surprised. Er—delighted!

Fiona I expect your toothache's *better* now, isn't it?

Agatha (*appalled*) Fiona! Will you behave yourself!

Mrs Hubback Thank you again, Mrs Hepworth. And you, too, Miss Francis.

Fiona Don't thank me. It wasn't *my* idea!

Mrs Hubback affects a painful jab of toothache, clutches her jaw and exits into the garden, suffering suitably

Fiona sits, dispiritedly, on the sofa

Fiona Agatha . . .

Agatha *Now* what?

Fiona Where am *I* suppose to sleep tonight?

Agatha How do I know? Down here, I expect.

Fiona Five hours on my backside at London Airport and when I do get here I haven't even got a bedroom——

Agatha You are a spoilsport! It's all part of the fun.

Julian (*enthusiastically*) Yes!

Agatha (*turning to Julian; losing her bonhomie*) A fine mess you got us into!

Julian (*plaintively*) I did leave a message for them about the plane.

Agatha A message? A message isn't enough! (*She turns away to the table* DR) Check and double-check, Mr Whittle. That's what we have to do in positions of responsibility. And that's what you're in, Mr Whittle, a position of responsibility. And you know what *we're* in, don't you?

Fiona *I* do. We're in the . . . !

Agatha I didn't ask you! (*To Julian*) Whatever we are in, Mr Whittle, you are the one who got us into it. And you are the one who is going to get us *out* of it!

Mario enters from the hall

They all watch his approach

Mario, a small Italian with limpid eyes—probably made more limpid by a few glasses of Chianti during the afternoon—gazes at Agatha, enraptured. He walks slowly across to her, stops in front of Agatha and looks at her with delight and deep admiration. Finally he speaks

Mario You . . . are a *won*derful woman.

Agatha is not sure how to take this. Finally she decides to introduce Fiona, and waves a hand in her direction

Agatha That's my sister over there—Fiona Francis.

Mario gives Fiona hardly a glance, dismissing her without interest

Mario She may be wonderful, too, for all I know. But I am talking about *you*. . . .

Agatha (*guardedly*) Oh, yes?

Mario I have heard all about you. (*He kisses the tips of his fingers expansively*)

Agatha Well, I only got here this afternoon——

Mario But already I know about you. Everybody knows about you. (*He turns to Julian*) She is a *won*derful woman.

Julian Oh, yes. Yes. Absolutely. Wonderful.

Mario (*to Agatha*) You hear him, what he say? He agree with me—you are a *won*derful woman. (*He holds out his hands to her*) Your-a hands, a-please.

Agatha looks doubtfully at Fiona, smiles nervously, and reluctantly gives him her hands

I kiss-a your hands. (*He kisses her hands lingeringly then turns to look at Julian again*) I kiss-a the hands of a *won*derful woman.

Julian Yes. I saw you.

Mario Have *you* done the same?

Julian Er . . . well, n-no, I haven't, actually. No. I . . . I just don't seem to have had the time.

Mario cannot believe his ears

Mario You come here, h'm?

Julian Oh. Er—right. (*He goes to Mario*)

Mario (*to Agatha*) Excuse me, please. (*To Julian*) You take-a these, please. (*He passes Agatha's hands to Julian*) Now—*you* kiss-a the hands of a *won*derful woman.

Agatha He doesn't have to do that!

Mario (*stopping her gently*) Please . . . (*To Julian*) Go ahead. You kiss-a the hands.

Julian Oh. Yes. Right. (*He tries to pluck up his courage*)

Agatha enjoys his embarrassment. Julian kisses Agatha quickly, once on each hand and moves away. Mario looks at him with pity. He smiles regretfully at Agatha

Mario These English ... they do not know how to kiss-a the hands.

Agatha And that's not the only thing Mr Whittle can't do. (*She glares at Julian*)

Mario suddenly drops to his knees and grabs Agatha, clinging to her like a limpet. Fiona and Julian look on in astonishment

Here! Get off! What do you think you're doing? Get off!

Mario releases her, but remains on his knees

Who *are* you, anyway?

Mario (*smiling proudly*) I am—Mario Marcello!

Julian He's the manager.

Agatha (*astonished*) The manager?! *You*?

Mario I cannot deny it. (*He gazes at her, smiling broadly*)

Agatha Well, where the hell have you been all the afternoon?

Mario (*delighted*) When you are angry you are even *more* wonderful!

Fiona Agatha, why don't you ask him about our room?

Agatha All right! All right! I'm going to. I haven't had the chance, have I? He's been kissing my hands.

Fiona (*piously*) I wouldn't let him kiss *my* hands ...

Agatha I didn't notice him asking to.

Fiona I wouldn't let a hotel manager kiss my hands. Not until he'd found me a bedroom, anyway.

Agatha Right then, Mr Marcello. What are you going to do about it?

Mario (*with a shrug*) No problem. I find you a room. (*He gets to his feet*)

Agatha When?

Mario No problem.

Agatha (*persisting*) When?

Mario Oh ... tomorrow. Maybe the next day——

Agatha Oh—domani! I've heard all about that. Never mind about domani. What about now?

Mario We have each other. We do not need a room.

Julian (*intervening diplomatically*) I know how you feel, Mario. I really do. And it's a nice sentiment, of course. And not surprising coming from an Italian. A very nice sentiment. Isn't it, Mrs Hepworth?

Agatha stares at Julian stonily

I think they'd prefer to have a room.

Mario gives a disappointed shrug

Mario All right. Very well. We get a room. (*To Agatha*) You are so wonderful I will give you anything you want. Anything!

Agatha A room will do very nicely, thank you.

Mario speaks quietly to Julian

Mario I think we have a little box-room for the sister.

Fiona I'm not sleeping in no box!

Mario (*patiently*) No, no. The box-room is where we keep the bags.

Julian laughs. Fiona glares at him. He stops laughing

Julian Sorry.

Mario It is all settled! (*To Fiona*) You will sleep in the box-room (*He turns to Agatha*) And you will sleep in *my* room. (*He smiles delightedly*)

Agatha (*looking aghast*) I'll do no such thing! You just listen to me, Mr Marcello. You go back to your office pronto, sort out your bookings and find a nice big room for me and my sister—*tonight!*

Mario (*with a helpless gesture*) Tonight is impossible. Tomorrow—maybe.

Agatha Never you mind "maybe". Domani definitely!

Mario (*to Julian*) You see what I mean? A *won*derful woman!

Mario exits into the hall, smiling

Agatha You'd better go with him, Mr Whittle. Though God knows it looks like a case of the blind leading the blind.

Julian Yes. Right. (*He starts to go, then looks back, imitating Mario*) Oh, you are a *won*derful woman!

Agatha reacts

Julian exits quickly into the hall

Agatha moves to sort out their luggage

Fiona I reckon he's after you.

Agatha Mr Whittle?!

Fiona No! That Eye-tie. I reckon he fancies you.

Agatha Don't be daft.

Fiona I've read about these Eye-ties. Anything female and moving and they're on to it. My friend warned me about foreigners, you know.

Agatha Oh, yes? (*She is busy with the bags*)

Fiona White slavers, half of them, she said.

Agatha White slavers? Talk sense.

Fiona It's true. Got to watch out when you're down on the beach. Put your sun-hat over your eyes for two minutes and the next thing you know you're in Morocco. (*She gets up and surveys the room, forlornly*) Oh, I can't sleep down here——

Agatha For heaven's sake where's your spirit of adventure?

Fiona I haven't got one.

Agatha Well, you'd better find one quick 'cos you're going to need it. (*She goes to Fiona to cheer her up a bit*) There's two nice comfy sofas here. We'll be as snug as bugs on these. Oh, it'll be fun, Fiona!

Fiona You call that fun?

Agatha (*romantically*) It'll be part of our holiday. Something to remember.

Fiona I'll remember all right. Remember not to come here again.

Agatha Just imagine getting back home and telling all your neighbours that you've actually slept the night on a sofa in the lounge of an Italian hotel! That's something none of *them* have ever done.

Fiona No. They've had more sense.

Agatha looks at Fiona pityingly

Agatha Why can't you enter into the spirit of the thing? It'll remind you of when you were a Girl Guide. You were always at your best under canvas.

Fiona (*giving sullen approval*) Oh . . . all right. (*She surveys the sofas*) Which one do *you* want?

Agatha I'll have the one up there. Then if there's a draught at least *you* won't be able to complain.

Fiona Right. I'll have this one, then.

Fiona goes to get her suitcase and small grip. She puts the suitcase on the table below the sofa and opens it. Agatha looks on in horror

Agatha What you doing?

Fiona Getting ready for bed, of course.

Agatha You haven't had your dinner yet.

Fiona I don't want no dinner. (*She starts unpacking*)

Agatha goes to her, quickly, to restrain her

Agatha You can't unpack *now*!

Fiona Why not?

Agatha Because this is the lounge, that's why not! Everyone'll be coming down for drinks. And after dinner they'll be in here with their coffee. Playing cards. Things like that.

Fiona (*defiantly*) I don't care *what* they're going to be doing. If this is my bedroom I'm going to unpack. (*She starts unpacking wildly, scattering her clothes all over the place*)

Agatha (*outraged*) People don't want to see your underwear all over the lounge!

Agatha tries to gather the clothes up and repack them again as fast as Fiona unpacks them. Finally they call it a truce, the place still partially littered with lingerie

Fiona picks up her small grip and starts to go towards the archway

Agatha *Now* where are you off to?

Fiona straightens herself and tries to look dignified

Fiona I'm going to change.

Agatha (*pleased*) Aaah! That's better! That's more like it. Put on a pretty frock and you'll be as right as ninepence.

Fiona Just out here, is it?

Agatha What?

Fiona The lavvy.

Agatha Oh—yes, love. Out there to the right. Only for God's sake don't go into the one with the picture of a man on the door.

Fiona exits into the hall

Agatha goes to her luggage to get a plastic bag containing a dress

Marisa enters through the glass doors, carrying a small tray from having just served drinks outside

Julian is following her closely

Marisa I cannot talk to you now. I am working.
Julian You're always working!
Agatha A pity *you* don't follow her example, Mr Whittle.
Julian (*seeing Agatha*) Ah—er—hullo, Mrs Hepworth.
Agatha And what were you doing out in the garden?
Marisa The same as he always does in the garden. (*She giggles at Julian and starts towards the hall*)
Agatha You were supposed to be sorting things out!
Julian Oh, *that*'s what it was! I knew there was something.

The Hubbacks come in from the garden. Hubback sees Marisa heading for the hall

Hubback Ah, Marisa! Just going swimming?
Mrs Hubback (*long-sufferingly*) Charles ...
Marisa Can I get you a drink?
Hubback (*beaming at her*) Yes, rather!
Mrs Hubback I'll have a dry sherry. What would *you* like, Charles?
Marisa Oh, *I* know what the Brigadier likes! (*She smiles wickedly*)

Marisa exits into the hall

Hubback is lost in admiration, watching her retreating legs

Mrs Hubback Charles ... Charles!
Hubback (*turning to his wife*) H'm?
Mrs Hubback (*pointedly*) I thought you were going to get Mrs Hepworth a drink ...
Hubback Was I? Ah! Yes. Of course. (*To Agatha*) Would you care for a ...?
Agatha No, thank you, dear. I'm just going to put my dress on in the toilet. You'll love it. It's sequins.
Hubback The toilet?

Agatha shows him the dress

Oh—the dress! Perhaps later on, then? H'm? When you're fully clothed and glittering.
Agatha (*grinning*) Cheeky!
Mrs Hubback Charles, you had something to say to Mrs Hepworth——
Hubback (*blankly*) What?

Mrs Hubback jerks her head towards Agatha a few times, trying to remind him

Ah. Yes. Quite right. Jolly good. Yes. Rather.
Agatha I beg your pardon?
Hubback (*moving nearer Agatha a little uncertainly*) Not very good at speeches, you understand, but I—er—, I—er—, I—er——
Julian (*to Agatha*) What's the matter with him?
Agatha I think he's going to lay an egg.
Mrs Hubback Oh, get on with it, Charles!

Hubback Yes. Wanted to say "thank you". The room, you know. Most considerate. Thoughtful. Kind. All that sort of thing.

Agatha Well, we couldn't go and spoil your holiday, now could we? Not on your last night.

Julian (*quietly*) If it *is* your last night ...

Agatha (*turning on him, severely*) It *will* be, won't it, Mr Whittle?

Julian Well, I hope so ...

Agatha It had better be more than "hope", Mr Whittle. You wouldn't like to see me angry, now would you?

Julian No fear!

Mrs Hubback Where will you and your sister be sleeping *tonight*, then, Mrs Hepworth?

Agatha In here, of course!

Mrs Hubback (*appalled*) In the lounge?

Agatha Well, there's nowhere else, is there?

Mrs Hubback Have you spoken to the manager about it?

Agatha Oh, yes.

Mrs Hubback And didn't *he* make a suggestion?

Agatha Yes, he did! Oh, don't you worry about us, dear. We'll be all right here for tonight. I'll be sleeping on the sofa over *there*—(*with relish*) right at the bottom of the stairs!

Mrs Hubback (*doomed*) Will you?

Agatha (*beaming, playfully, at Hubback*) Oh, yes! So there'll be no chance of you getting up early, creeping down the stairs and going off to the beach without me, will there?

Hubback Won't there?

Agatha Oh, no! 'Cos I'll already be down here—just *waiting* for you!

The Hubbacks look at each other in alarm

Fiona enters from the hall, dressed not for dinner but for bed. She is wearing a long nightdress, and her hair is in curlers. She carries her grip, a pillow, a blanket and an old teddy bear. She takes no notice of anyone, but walks straight to the sofa DL, lies down and arranges the blanket over her legs. Then she looks at them all for the first time

Fiona Goodnight, everyone! (*She turns on her side and pulls the blanket up over her shoulders, ready for sleep*)

Agatha is mortified

The others remain frozen, unable to believe their eyes

Black-out

The CURTAIN *falls*

ACT II

SCENE 1

The same. The following morning. It is peaceful and hot with the cicadas rattling madly in the trees outside

Fiona is asleep under the blankets on her sofa

When the CURTAIN rises, Marisa, in her bikini and carrying a beach towel, is coming down the stairs just as she did at the beginning of the play. She walks across the lounge and out through the glass doors to the swimming pool

No sooner has she gone than Hubback comes down the stairs in hot pursuit

At the same moment, Julian comes in from the hall in similar urgent fashion. They are both wearing bathing trunks and beach shoes, and each carries a rolled-up beach towel. Hubback is wearing a Panama hat. Julian sees Hubback ahead of him and stops, rather put out

Julian Ah! Brigadier!

Hubback stops. He turns and sees Julian

Hubback Ah! Whittle!

A brief pause. They look at each other, uncertainly

You got us a flight back to London?
Julian Ah. No. Not yet. I . . . I'm just working on it.
Hubback (*looking at Julian doubtfully*) H'm. I *thought* you looked busy. (*He glances, furtively, towards the swimming pool, where no doubt Marisa is already disporting herself*) Well . . . don't let me keep you.

Julian looks at him, blankly

Julian What?
Hubback From your work, Whittle!
Julian Ah—no, of course not.

Hubback takes another look poolwards

Are you . . . thinking of going for a swim?

Hubback looks at him blankly, as if the idea had never crossed his mind

Hubback What?

Julian I—I just wondered if you had any ... thoughts along those lines.
Hubback Hadn't really considered it.
Julian Oh? (*He glances down at Hubback's bathing trunks*) It's just that—seeing you like ... like that—I thought possibly swimming was not too far from your mind.
Hubback What? (*He looks down at his trunks as if seeing them for the first time*) Oh, these? Yes. Yes, I see what you mean.
Julian Exactly. You do look like a man going swimming.
Hubback (*thoughtfully*) Do I?
Julian Oh, yes.
Hubback Good lord. ... (*Pause*) No. No, I'm ... I'm going walking, as a matter of fact.
Julian (*as if that explained the trunks*) I knew it was one or the other!

Pause

Hubback Er—*you* weren't thinking of ... er ...?
Julian Good Lord, no!
Hubback I just wondered.
Julian No. I'm working. (*He smiles*) You're walking and I'm working!

They both give a little self-conscious laugh

Fiona rises from beneath the blanket on the sofa

Fiona Whatever's going on?

Hubback and Julian turn and look in surprise at the apparition

Hubback Oh, my God!
Fiona Here—what you doing in my bedroom? And with no clothes on!

They look at each other, then down and realize their predicament. In unison they both allow their towels to unroll like blinds to conceal their bathing trunks

Fiona *I* never rang for Room Service.
Julian Haven't you had breakfast?
Fiona I haven't had dinner yet.
Julian It's too late for that. They're doing breakfast now.   ·
Fiona Here! You're not going into breakfast dressed like that, are you?
Julian No, no—we've *had* breakfast. You've had breakfast, haven't you, Brigadier?
Hubback Yes—rather! Had it up in our room.
Fiona It's not *your* room, it's *our* room! You've just got the loan of it.
Hubback Ah—yes—you're quite right, of course. (*He moves towards her*) And I must tell you how——
Fiona Don't you come near me! (*She cowers, clutching the blanket to her*)
Hubback I was only going to say——
Fiona Keep away! I've heard all about Army men. I know what they're like. All they think about is plunder, pillage and rape.
Julian Plunder, pillage and rape? Don't be silly. He was in the Queen's Own. (*He enjoys the joke*)

Hubback glares at him, and then sidles towards the glass doors

Hubback Well, I . . . I think I'll just go and see if she's still there.
Julian What?
Hubback (*covering quickly*) See if it's still there!
Julian See if *what*'s still there?
Hubback Oh, the—er—the beach. Cliffs. That sort of thing. Yes. Right.

Hubback stumbles out through the glass doors in confusion

Fiona He's acting very furtive for an Army man.
Julian Yes, he is, isn't he? Very furtive.
Fiona I expect he's up to something.
Julian I wouldn't be surprised. (*He looks, enviously, after Hubback*)
Fiona I wonder if his wife knows.
Julian She's probably used to it by now.
Fiona Are *you* married, Mr Whittle?
Julian (*turning to Fiona*) Certainly not!
Fiona Did you never think of it?
Julian Yes, I thought of it. Then I thought *better* of it.
Fiona (*reflectively*) It's a funny thing, isn't it?
Julian What is?
Fiona Well—you know—sex.
Julian Oh, that. Yes, it is funny sometimes. (*He chuckles, thoughtfully, at a particular memory*)
Fiona I mean, some people seem to go in for it and others don't fancy it at all.
Julian (*surprised*) Not at all? Good Lord . . .
Fiona Well—like my sister Agatha. I don't suppose it ever crosses her mind.
Julian It must have crossed her mind once.
Fiona Why?
Julian Because she was married!
Fiona Oh, that had nothing to do with sex.
Julian No?
Fiona Oh, no. That was Old Time Dancing.
Julian Old Time Dancing?
Fiona That's what they had in common. Every Tuesday and Saturday. Oh, you should have seen them . . . !
Julian I wish I had!
Fiona Their tango was the talk of the town. Agatha was always at her best with a number on her back. (*She sighs*) It was a pity they ever stopped doing it.
Julian I thought you said they never *started* doing it.
Fiona No, no! Not sex. Old Time Dancing.
Julian Oh, I see. Well, why did they?
Fiona He started drinking too much cider and lost his sense of balance.
Julian What a pity. They might have been on the telly.
Fiona Do you *always* wear bathing trunks when you're working?
Julian What? (*He remembers*) Good Lord! I'd forgotten all about them. I'll take them off.

Fiona No! (*She hides her face in the blanket*)
Julian All right! All right! Don't panic. I'm not taking them off in here.

Fiona emerges cautiously

   Isn't it time you got out of bed?
Fiona I'm not sure if I can.
Julian What?
Fiona I've got pins and needles!
Julian Oh, my God . . .!

Fiona attempts to get out of bed and cries out in pain

Fiona Oooooh!
Julian What's the matter?
Fiona (*poised*) I can't put my foot down! Here—quick! Help me!

*Julian goes to help her. She holds on to him with one arm around his neck. He
supports her around the waist while she tries to put one foot on the ground*

Julian Go on—put it on the ground! Put your foot down!
Fiona I can't!
Julian Put it down!
Fiona (*putting her foot down*) Oooooh! (*She cries out and clings on to him.
   They lose their balance and fall on to the sofa*)

   *Agatha enters from the hall and sees them. She is wearing a lurid floral
   dress, white plimsolls and her sun-hat*

Agatha Mr Whittle!

*Julian and Fiona struggle to sort themselves out. They finally succeed and
stand side by side facing Agatha. Agatha is frozen to the spot, appalled by the
sight before her. Fiona slowly and surreptitiously picks up the beach towel that
Julian has dropped in the melee and passes it to him, her eyes on Agatha.
Julian takes the towel and holds it across in front of his middle as if he is about
to do a conjuring trick*

   Well, Mr Whittle? Is this what you mean by giving service to your clients?
Julian We were just going to put our clothes on.
Agatha I can't think what you were doing in my sister's bedroom with your
   clothes off in the first place.
Julian No, neither can I!
Fiona He was helping me.
Agatha Helping *himself*, too, I shouldn't wonder.
Julian I was only helping her to put her feet on the ground.
Agatha (*grinning*) Couldn't she manage that on her own?
Fiona They were asleep.
Agatha I'm not surprised. So are you half the time. Oh, for heaven's sake,
   go and put your clothes on before the entire male population of Italy gets
   out of control.

Fiona crosses towards the archway, wrapped in her blanket

And don't be long about it, 'cos we're all going down to the beach in a minute.

Fiona (*grumbling*) I haven't had my breakfast yet.

Agatha Well, don't hang about. I've told everyone we're playing cricket.

On her way out, Fiona turns

Fiona (*proudly*) I had two men in my bedroom just now.

Agatha Oh, yes?

Fiona And neither of them had their clothes on!

Fiona exits into the hall, the blanket around her, carrying her small grip

Agatha (*grinning at Julian*) If she's like that now, what'll she be like at the end of a fortnight? I'd better get this lot tidied up. (*She moves to fasten Fiona's suitcase*) There weren't many people down to breakfast this morning.

Julian I'm not surprised . . . !

Agatha What do you mean?

Julian (*evasively*) Well—most of them had breakfast in their rooms today.

Agatha Oh, I see. Is that what they *always* do?

Julian Well . . . not in such great numbers.

Agatha What was so different today, then?

Julian (*trying to be tactful*) Well, Mrs Hepworth, I suppose it could be . . . well . . . because of what happened last night in the dining-room.

Agatha Last night?

Julian Yes. During dinner. You remember.

Agatha (*remembering*) Oh, that! I thought that was rather fun. (*She goes and puts Fiona's suitcase with hers*)

Julian (*following Agatha*) Yes. Yes, I know you did, Mrs Hepworth. I know you did. But, you see, it was the first time they'd had community singing during dinner.

Agatha Well, the service was so slow I thought a couple of choruses of "Boiled Beef and Carrots" would help to pass the time. (*She goes to get Fiona's pillow*)

Julian (*following her*) Yes. Yes, I know you did, Mrs Hepworth. And it did. It did pass the time. But I don't think they particularly wanted to sing "Boiled Beef and Carrots". Not with a plateful of pasta.

Agatha Oh, I see. . . . Well, of course, I won't do that every night.

Julian (*relieved*) Oh, good!

Agatha No. We can take it in turns to choose the songs.

Mario comes in through the glass doors, searching. He sees Agatha and smiles joyfully

Mario Aaaaaaah! There you are—— (*He crosses towards her, his smile a mile wide*)

Agatha What do *you* want?

Mario I have been looking for you everywhere. (*He holds his hands out to her*) Your hands, a-please.

Agatha Oh, no! Not that again.

Mario Please——

Reluctantly Agatha gives her hands to him. Mario bends over them and kisses them lingeringly. Julian laughs. Agatha looks at him sharply

Agatha I don't know what you're laughing about, Mr Whittle. It's your turn next! (*She throws the pillow at him abruptly*)
Julian Oh, no! Not this time. I've got work to do. Besides, I'm not dressed to kiss-a the hands.

Julian goes, hastily, through the archway, carrying the pillow and struggling to keep his towel in position

Mario, bent over Agatha's hands, looks up at her with a smile

Mario You are a *won*derful woman.
Agatha Yes, I know. You told me.
Mario But, you did not come to my room last night.
Agatha No, I certainly did not!
Mario (*incredulously*) You prefer to sleep down here? With your *sister*?
Agatha Yes, I do, thank you very much.
Mario Oh, I love-a the English women!
Agatha I'm sure you do. Well, there are plenty of *young* English girls staying here, so you'd better go after them. Let go of my hands!
Mario Ah! You are frightened that your husband will suddenly walk in?
Agatha You'd have a hell of a surprise if he did!
Mario Why? He is a big, strong man?
Agatha Not any more. He's dead.
Mario (*mortified*) Oh, I am so sorry——
Agatha Well, don't go bursting into tears about it.
Mario I did not know. (*Sympathetically*) Let me kiss-a your hands——
Agatha You don't have to keep kissing my hands every five minutes!
Mario You realize something?
Agatha *Now* what?
Mario *You* have no husband—*I* have no wife. So—(*He goes abruptly down on to one knee in front of her*) *you* will be my wife!
Agatha I'll be nothing of the sort! Get up at once!

Mario grabs her firmly around the knees. Agatha totters, unsteadily

What do you think you're doing? Leave go of me! (*She loses her balance*) Oooh!

Agatha collapses onto the sofa with Mario on top of her

Mrs Hubback comes down the stairs and sees them. She reacts, appalled

Mrs Hubback Mr Marcello!

Agatha sees Mrs Hubback and pushes Mario away, causing him to fall face down on the floor. Mrs Hubback surveys the scene in astonishment

I was looking for my husband.

Agatha (*trying to ignore Mario at her feet*) Perhaps he's gone for a walk, dear.

Mrs Hubback Yes. I expect so.

Mario stirs faintly, raises his head and looks at Mrs Hubback. Mrs Hubback looks down at him

Good morning, Mr Marcello.

Mario (*waving feebly*) Buon giorno.

Mrs Hubback No sign of an aircraft, I suppose?

Mario (*blankly*) You are looking for one?

Mrs Hubback (*patiently*) Yes, Mr Marcello. We are looking for one.

Mario (*shrugging*) Maybe you find one at the airport.

Mrs Hubback We are not looking for a random aircraft, Mr Marcello, but for a specific one. One on which, by the good offices of yourself or Mr Whittle, reservations have been made to transport myself and my husband back to the United Kingdom.

Mario I see . . .

Mrs Hubback Good. Then may I suggest that you collect yourself up from the floor of Mrs Hepworth's temporary bedroom with all convenient speed and hastily remove your ass to your office!

Mario rises slowly to his feet, gazing at her in wonder, a big smile of delight spreading across his face

Mario Oh, *you* are a wonderful woman, too! You are both wonderful women!

Mario exits into the hall

Mrs Hubback (*to Agatha*) You can imagine what they were like during the war.

Agatha goes eagerly to Mrs Hubback, anxious to keep off the subject of Mario's behaviour a moment ago

Agatha Now, dear—you tell me! What's your favourite position?

Mrs Hubback (*not comprehending*) I beg your pardon?

Agatha (*laughing*) On the field!

Mrs Hubback What *are* you talking about?

Agatha (*beaming with joy*) We're all going to play cricket down on the beach!

Mrs Hubback (*appalled*) Oh, no, we're not!

Agatha Oh, yes, we are!

Mrs Hubback Mrs Hepworth, I will *not* be playing cricket.

Agatha (*smiling, broadly*) 'Course you will, dear. We'll *all* be playing. Even the vicar. I've been rounding people up ever since breakfast!

Marisa comes running in from the pool, giggling and out of breath, carrying her beach towel

Hubback, red-faced, follows her in closely

Marisa No, no—you must not chase me any more!

Hubback I almost caught you that time!

Marisa and Hubback stop when they see Agatha and Mrs Hubback facing them grimly, and their laughter peters out

Marisa Your husband has been chasing me all over the beach.
Mrs Hubback (*looking, balefully, at Hubback*) Yes, I'm sure he has.
Hubback Well, I didn't catch her. (*Quietly*) More's the pity.
Marisa I was too fast for him. (*She giggles at Hubback and crosses towards the archway*)
Mrs Hubback That doesn't surprise me.
Agatha (*moving to Hubback*) And where were you hiding yourself at breakfast this morning, Major?
Hubback Hiding? Good Lord, I wasn't hiding! Whatever gave you that idea? Just decided to have it in our room, that's all. It was my wife, you see. She felt a little peculiar.
Agatha Yes. I can see she doesn't look too good.
Mrs Hubback I beg your pardon?
Agatha But we'll soon put the roses back—down there on the beach! (*To Hubback*) And now *you've* had a bit of running practice you'll be all ready to go racing after the ball, won't you?
Hubback Ah . . .
Mrs Hubback Well—actually—er—we *were* thinking of . . . of popping into the village. Weren't we, Charles?
Hubback Ah! Yes. Popping into the village. Something I've got to buy.
Agatha What?
Hubback Pardon?
Agatha What is it that you want to buy?
Hubback (*thinking quickly*) What is it that I want to buy . . . ? Er—shaving cream!
Agatha Right. Here you are.

To Hubback's surprise, Agatha promptly produces a tube of shaving cream from her bag

Hubback Shaving cream . . .
Agatha I heard you say last night that you needed some, so I went down there before breakfast so as not to waste any time.

The Hubbacks exchange a look

Hubback Well, that was very kind of you. Wasn't it, darling? Yes. Very kind. (*He takes the shaving cream tentatively, then thinks of a way out*) Oh, what a pity!
Agatha What?
Hubback This is brushless. I always use lather. (*He smiles triumphantly*)
Agatha Well, I wasn't sure, so I got both!

Hubback's face falls as Agatha produces a second tube and holds it out to him with a big smile. Marisa laughs. Hubback takes the shaving cream

Mrs Hubback (*impatiently*) Oh, for heaven's sake, Charles—come and put
your clothes on! You look ridiculous.
Hubback Oh. Yes. Right.

Mrs Hubback starts to pull him towards the stairs

Agatha Don't you be long now! (*With a big smile*) I'll be waiting for you.
Hubback Yes, I'm sure you will——

Mrs Hubback goes up the stairs

Hubback turns to Marisa

I'll catch you next time!
Mrs Hubback (*off*) Charles!
Hubback Coming, dear! Coming!

Hubback exits upstairs

Marisa and Agatha laugh

Marisa The Brigadier—he is a very naughty man!
Agatha They're all the same, dear. He's as bad as that manager out there.
All sex-mad, if you ask me. And the older they are, the worse they get.
You take my advice, Marisa—never get married if you're a woman!

*Fiona comes in from the hall. She is now wearing a shapeless plain dress,
plimsolls and a cardigan, and carries her grip and a copy of "Woman's
Own"*

Oh, good. You've got your clothes on again. Now all the men can feel
safe.
Fiona Funny sort of breakfast, wasn't it?
Agatha What do you mean?
Fiona Just coffee and rolls.
Agatha That's Continental, that is. What's wrong with it?
Fiona In Eastcliffe you get porridge or fruit juice with egg, bacon, sausage
and fried bread to follow.
Agatha But you're not in Eastcliffe, are you? Can't you acquire a little
panache?
Fiona And no proper marmalade . . .
Agatha Well, you packed your pot of Golden Shred, didn't you?
Fiona Yes, I know I did. But I didn't dare take it out of my handbag. Not in
front of the waiter.
Marisa (*beginning to leave*) Well, I must go and take off my bikini.
Agatha That won't take long, will it, dear? (*She chuckles*)

Marisa exits into the hall

Agatha What a sweet girl she is, isn't she? Always so happy and smiling. I
like to see people happy and smiling. (*She turns and comes face to face
with Fiona, the picture of misery*) Oh, my God . . .! You'd better put
that over there with the rest of our luggage.

Fiona (*as she goes*) Yes. And I hope I'm going to be in a *proper* room tonight—— (*She puts her grip with the other cases*)

Agatha watches her as she returns, intrigued by the cardigan she is wearing

Agatha You sure you're going to be warm enough in that cardigan?

Fiona (*fingering the cardigan, fondly*) I bought this when we were thinking of going to West Wittering.

Agatha But we didn't go to West Wittering, did we?

Fiona I don't care. I'm not going to waste *my* money. (*She wanders away towards the table* DR) I don't feel very well. . . . I think I'll just sit here and read my *Woman's Own*. (*She sits down*)

Agatha You didn't come hundreds of miles to sit indoors and read your *Woman's Own*! You could have stayed at home and done that. Oh, this is all I need . . . !

Fiona (*with a voice of doom*) I bet it's happening to *me*, Agatha.

Agatha What's happening to you?

Fiona The same as happened to that woman I told you about. Bit by a bug, she was. Passed right away.

Agatha But you haven't been bitten by a bug!

Fiona How do I know? How can I be sure?

Agatha Because you'd have felt something.

Fiona It could have happened in the night when I was asleep. I told you we should have had mosquito nets.

Agatha You were all right earlier on, weren't you? Oh, yes! You were all right then, when you had naked men dancing about in here! What happened, for heaven's sake?

Fiona Nothing. They put their clothes back on.

Agatha Not the men! What happened to *you*?

Fiona Oh. I dunno. I went all peculiar.

Agatha You didn't have far to go.

Fiona Do you think I'm going to die, Agatha?

Agatha I shouldn't be surprised. You might at least have waited to die till we got back home.

Fiona (*rummaging in her handbag*) Perhaps I'd better take one of those pills. . . .

Agatha Don't be daft! I told you they're for travel sickness.

Fiona Maybe that's what I've got.

Agatha You've only walked from here to the toilet! You can't call that travelling.

Fiona Perhaps it's delayed action. Perhaps I'm paying now for yesterday.

Agatha It's not you that's paying, it's me! And this is all the thanks I get.

Fiona It's not my fault if I'm ill. I think I'd better go and lie down on my bed. (*She goes to lie down on her "bed"*)

Agatha Yes, I should if I were you. If you're going to die you may as well do it in comfort. (*She goes to get a cricket bat from the corner seat above the archway*)

Julian peers in through the archway. He is now dressed. He does not see Agatha or Fiona

Julian Marisa . . . (*He comes in, cautiously, and goes towards the glass doors*)

Agatha watches him, unobserved

Marisa——
Agatha Mr Whittle!

Julian jumps with fright, turns and sees Agatha

Julian I—I didn't see you there.
Agatha No. I should think you didn't. Got your mind on other things, haven't you? Well, have you found us a room yet?
Julian Er—no—not yet. But I'm working on it.
Agatha You didn't look as if you were working on it!
Julian Well, I will! I'll go and work on it now. (*He starts to go, crossing below her*)
Agatha Oh, no, you won't!
Julian (*stopping nervously*) I thought you wanted me to?
Agatha You can work on it this afternoon. This morning you're playing cricket! (*She smiles at him, encouragingly*)
Julian Well . . . actually . . . I really would rather work——
Agatha (*firmly*) You're playing cricket! (*She thrusts the bat into his hands*)
Julian Oh, very well. I'll open the batting.
Agatha No, you won't—*I'*m doing that! (*She grabs the bat back again*)

The Hubbacks creep downstairs and head for the glass doors

Agatha (*sensing the Hubbacks are behind her*) You going somewhere, Major?

The Hubbacks stop, furtively, and turn to see Agatha. They feign surprise

Hubback Ah! there you are, Mrs Hepworth! We were looking for you. I was just saying to my wife, "Let's keep an eye out for Mrs Hepworth." Wasn't I, Audrey? (*He gets a bleak look from his wife*) Yes. . . . And she said, "What a good idea, darling!" Didn't you, Audrey? (*He gets another bleak look*) Yes! So we came downstairs—quite quickly, as a matter of fact— and that's what we were doing—looking for *you*.
Agatha (*crossing to Hubback*) Well, you wouldn't find me out there, would you?
Mrs Hubback We couldn't be certain *where* you were——
Agatha But I said I'd be in here, didn't I?
Hubback (*a bit too surprised*) Did you? In here? Good Lord. . . .
Agatha Don't say you'd forgotten?
Hubback Well, I . . .
Agatha (*playfully*) That's the second time you've forgotten arrangements, isn't it? I am surprised at you. An Army man forgetting his rendezvous. (*She sticks the cricket bat under his nose*) Anyway—what about that?
Hubback I beg your pardon?
Agatha Do you know what it is?
Hubback Well, it's . . . er . . . er . . .
Mrs Hubback (*quietly*) Cricket bat.

Hubback Yes. Cricket bat. Small cricket bat. Bit *too* small for me, I'd say.
Agatha You'll have to bend your knees, then, won't you?
Hubback Sorry?
Mrs Hubback Did you buy it in the village?
Agatha Buy it? I borrowed it. Someone left it out there in the hall, so I've
    borrowed it.
Fiona That's stealing, that is. . . .

They all look across at the recumbent form on the sofa

Agatha Oh, you're still alive, then? The way you were going on I thought
    you'd have sprouted wings and gone to Heaven by now.
Mrs Hubback Isn't your sister feeling very well, Mrs Hepworth?
Agatha Don't encourage her. She thinks she's dying, but she'll be all right in
    a minute.

*Mrs Hubback crosses to Fiona, sensing an avenue of escape from the sporting
activities*

Mrs Hubback Oh, dear. What seems to be the trouble, Miss Francis?
Fiona I don't know. But I'm far from my best.
Agatha You haven't been near your best for years.
Mrs Hubback Well, we mustn't leave you here on your own. I'll stay and
    look after you.
Agatha You can't do that!
Mrs Hubback But I don't mind, really.
Agatha It's quite all right, Mrs Hubback dear. Fiona's coming with us. It'll
    do her good.
Mrs Hubback But is that wise? In her condition. I'm quite happy to stay
    here.
Julian
Hubback } (*together*) { So am I!
Agatha (*undeterred*) Oh, no. We're *all* going! Come on, Fiona!

Reluctantly, Fiona sits up and sees the men

Fiona Oo! There are two men in my bedroom again!
Agatha Well, mark it in your diary because it won't happen often.
Fiona They've got their clothes on this time . . .
Agatha Don't sound so disappointed

    *Mario comes in through the archway. He is now dressed for cricket in white
    shirt and trousers, and is smiling broadly*

They all look at him in surprise

Mrs Hubback Mr Marcello! What do you think you're doing?
Mario I come to play cricket with the *won*derful women!
Agatha Oh, good! Come on, then, everybody! Let's go down to the beach
    and find the others. They'll be wondering where we've got to. They said
    they'd keep an eye out for us.

Julian Yes, I bet they will ...!
Agatha What was that, Mr Whittle?
Julian Oh—nothing!
Agatha You all right, Fiona?
Fiona (*the martyr*) I suppose so ...
Agatha You got your sun-hat?
Fiona Yes.
Agatha Well, put it on, then. We don't want you catching sunstroke on top of everything else, do we? Oh, I *am* going to enjoy myself! (*She beams, happily, at everyone*)
Mario (*to Mrs Hubback*) She is a *won*derful woman. And so are *you*! Both wonderful women! (*He embraces her*)
Mrs Hubback (*appalled*) Do you mind! (*She frees herself, hastily*)
Agatha Right! Come on, then, everybody—off we go! Mr Whittle—you look after Mrs Hubback—all right? And Mr Marcello—did you remember the cricket ball?

Mario takes a cricket ball out of his pocket and holds it aloft

Oh, well done! I knew I could rely on you. You lead the way to the beach, Admiral! You can't miss it—it's the yellow bit before you get to the sea! (*She laughs, raucously*)

They all exit, reluctantly, through the glass doors, muttering complaints as they go

Come on, Fiona! Don't hang about.

Fiona starts to go, reluctantly

Fiona (*grumbling*) I wish we'd gone to Eastcliffe same as last year ...
Agatha Fiona Francis, I'm telling you for positively the last time—I don't want to hear no more about Eastcliffe! You understand? I'm sick of the sound of it. And I'm sick of you going about with a long face. You're on your holidays! You've come out here to *enjoy* yourself. (*With grim determination*) And *I'm* going to see that you do!

With cricket bat aloft, Agatha propels Fiona out through the glass doors to the beach

The music swells

The CURTAIN falls

SCENE 2

The same. Early evening. It is getting dark outside and the electric lights are on

When the CURTAIN *rises, Marisa, wearing a pretty dress, is putting up some paper decorations*

Julian looks in from the hall and sees Marisa. He tiptoes up behind her and is just about to put his arms around her waist

Marisa No, Mr Whittle ...
Julian You must have radar!
Marisa I am working. (*She moves away, playing it cool*)
Julian You're *always* working!
Marisa I have to get everything ready for this evening.
Julian (*following her*) What's so special about this evening?
Marisa The carnival! Had you forgotten? Tonight there will be music and dancing—and a lot of fireworks out there.
Julian Well, what about some fireworks in *here*?

Julian tries to embrace Marisa again, but she eludes him, enjoying playing it cool

Marisa No. I am too busy.
Julian Oh, come on! They'll all be back for dinner soon.
Marisa I thought you would be tired after your game of cricket on the beach.
Julian No. I didn't stay there very long.
Marisa You mean you managed to escape from Mrs Hepworth?
Julian Well, I only scored five and dropped two catches so she was glad to get rid of me. Any message from the airport?
Marisa No.
Julian If Mrs Hepworth has to spend another night down here she'll probably kill me——
Marisa You must try not to think about that. Think about something else.
Julian (*with a grin*) What a good idea. Come and sit down!

He grabs Marisa quickly and they fall onto the sofa, a giggling, struggling mass

Hubback enters from the hall. He looks very hot and breathless. He has his binoculars hanging from his neck and is carrying a large piece of hardboard and a small branch that is roughly the shape of an officer's baton. He sees Julian and Marisa and reacts

Hubback Working, Whittle?
Julian Just getting a little job satisfaction. (*He rises, below the sofa*)

Marisa tries to control her giggles and moves away a little. Hubback puts his "baton" and hardboard down on the padded seat UL, *then returns to Marisa*

Hubback Lucky I came in when I did. God knows what would have happened.
Julian (*ruefully*) Yes, and now he's the only one who *will* know!

Hubback consoles Marisa with a nauseatingly paternal smirk

Hubback You—er—you all right, are you, my dear?

Marisa Yes, thank you, Charlie.

Hubback Good. Good. Little thing like you. . . . Want to watch out for beasts like Whittle. Lucky I was here, eh? You can always rely on the Army to be in the right place at the right time.

Julian What? Even the Queen's Own?

Julian and Marisa laugh. Hubback glares at Julian, then returns his attention to Marisa

Hubback You should have called out for help.

Julian I didn't need any help.

Hubback No, I bet you didn't! Beast. . . . (*He turns to Marisa*) Still, no bones broken, eh? All in one piece? (*He starts to pat her shoulders and arms rather extensively*)

Julian You don't have to check!

Hubback has the good grace to look a little sheepish

Hubback Well, now—is there any sign of Miss Francis?

Julian and Marisa look puzzled

Marisa Miss Francis? No, she is not up here. I have not seen her since this morning.

Hubback (*to Julian, importantly*) We rang reception, of course.

Julian Did you?

Hubback Oh, yes. Put them in the picture. Got to keep checking, though. (*He looks out of the glass doors with his binoculars*)

Julian and Marisa exchange a puzzled look

Julian What are you talking about? Why should Miss Francis be up here when the rest of you were down there?

Hubback looks at Julian, the weight of responsibility heavy on his shoulders

Hubback You mean to say you haven't heard?

Julian Heard what?

Hubback About Miss Francis.

Julian No. Has something happened to her?

Hubback It certainly has. We've lost the bloody woman.

Julian and Marisa gaze at him in astonishment

Julian Lost her? What do you mean?

Hubback Well, one minute she was there, the next minute she'd disappeared.

Julian I expect she just got tired of cricket. Went for a walk.

Hubback That's what *we* thought. At first. But we searched the whole of the beach and she was nowhere to be found.

Julian (*crossing to Hubback, astonished*) You searched all of the beach?

Hubback Well, what the hell do you think we've been doing all the afternoon?
Julian I thought you'd still be playing cricket.
Hubback No such luck. While you were up here doing—(*with a glance at Marisa*)—whatever it was *you* were doing, we were all racing up and down the scorching bloody sand trying to find Miss Francis!

Julian laughs

It's not funny, Whittle!
Julian Oh. Sorry. I thought it was.
Marisa When did you realize that Miss Francis was missing?
Hubback At lunchtime.
Marisa But it is nearly seven o'clock now! You mean she has been lost for six hours?
Hubback Yes!
Julian And you've been searching all that time?
Hubback Mrs Hepworth didn't give us much choice.
Julian No, I bet she didn't!
Marisa I will get you a drink, Charlie. You look as if you are ready for one.
Hubback Ah. Yes. Good idea. Gin and tonic. Thank you.

Marisa disappears through the archway

Hubback watches her go, then realizes that Julian is watching him watch her, and covers, quickly moving to the sofa

Oh! What a day! (*He sits down*) I'm exhausted.
Julian If I'd known I'd have helped.
Hubback Yes. I'm sure you would. Well, I'll tell you one thing, Whittle. I wish *you'd* been down there doing what *I* was doing, and I'd been up here doing what *you* were doing!

Agatha and Mrs Hubback come in from the hall. They are arm-in-arm, and Mrs Hubback is carrying the cricket bat over one shoulder. Agatha has caught the sun a bit. She is moaning quietly, and Mrs Hubback is comforting her

Agatha Oh, dear. . . . Oh, dear. . . .
Mrs Hubback There, there, there. . . .

Hubback gets to his feet quickly

Agatha (*looking at Julian despairingly*) You've heard the news, I take it?
Julian Yes. The Brigadier put me in the picture.
Agatha You realize then that by now my sister could be halfway to Morocco?
Julian (*looking puzzled*) Morocco?
Agatha Well, that's where they take them, isn't it?
Julian Who?
Agatha White slavers!

Julian Don't be silly! No self-respecting white slaver would want to ... (*he peters out*) Oh, surely not? I expect she went for a walk.

Agatha Fiona wouldn't walk across the road if she could help it. Anyhow, she disappeared at lunchtime. If she's been walking she'll be halfway to Monte Carlo by now.

Hubback You mustn't worry, Mrs Hepworth. She'll turn up. Presumably she knows the name of this hotel?

Agatha She'll have forgotten it by now!

Marisa enters with a gin and tonic from the hall

Hubback holds out his hand to receive it

Oh, that is sweet of you, dear. I *am* a bit thirsty. (*She takes the drink and downs quite a lot of it*)

Hubback watches in horror as his gin disappears, his hand still outstretched hopefully

(*Moving to Mrs Hubback*) There you are, Mrs Hubback dear. You have a sip of that.

Mrs Hubback takes the drink

Hubback lets his hand fall

Agatha smiles at Mrs Hubback

After all, you do deserve it, don't you? You know, they'll have you playing for England soon. I bet you're proud of her, aren't you, Major?

Hubback suffers in silence

(*To Mrs Hubback*) I didn't think you had it in you!

Mrs Hubback Well, one mustn't always go by outside appearances. (*She hands the gin back to Agatha*) Thank you.

Agatha No, no—I've had enough, dear.

Hubback (*helpfully*) *I* don't mind finishing it off.

Agatha goes and hands him what is left of his drink. He sees nothing left, puts the glass down, gloomily, and breaks away DL

Agatha (*returning to Mrs Hubback*) I was surprised enough when you hit your first ball for six, but when you went on to get fifty—well, I never!

Mrs Hubback Well, I didn't go to Cheltenham Ladies College for nothing, you know. (*She essays a stroke with the cricket bat*)

Agatha (*smiling*) Oh, yes. I thought you'd played before. I could tell. You had style. You know what I mean? (*She looks severely at Julian*) *You* didn't do too well, did you, Mr Whittle?

Julian Well, I had other things on my mind.

Hubback (*quietly*) Yes, you certainly did! Dirty beast ...!

Marisa I am sorry to hear about your sister, Mrs Hepworth. But I am sure she will be all right.

Agatha Thank you, dear. I hope so. (*Anxiously*) I just wish I knew what had happened to her——

Hubback We'll soon find her, don't you worry. Always rely on the infantry.

Agatha (*going to Marisa*) The Colonel's got every male holidaymaker for miles around all helping in the search. (*Turning to glare at Julian*) And you know something, Mr Whittle? They're all volunteers.

Julian Yes. I bet they are. You, you and you!

Marisa But, Mrs Hepworth, your sister may not be lost at all.

Agatha (*sweetly logical*) If she wasn't lost she'd be *here*, now wouldn't she, dear?

Mrs Hubback She's probably just doing a bit of shopping.

Agatha For six hours? She wouldn't even spend six hours in Marks and Spencer's.

Mrs Hubback You really mustn't worry. I'm sure they'll find her, Mrs Hepworth.

Agatha crosses back to Mrs Hubback

Agatha Oh, look, dear—you can't go on calling me "Mrs Hepworth". Not now we're team-mates! Call me Agatha.

Mrs Hubback What?

Agatha Agatha. That's my name. Agatha.

Mrs Hubback (*reluctantly*) Oh. Oh, very well . . . Agatha.

Agatha And what's *your* name?

Mrs Hubback Er . . . Audrey.

Agatha Oh, good. So from now on it's "Audrey" and "Agatha"—okay?

Mrs Hubback (*without enthusiasm*) Very well. Audrey and Agatha . . .

Hubback (*quietly*) Oh, my God. . . . I wish I'd got a drink.

Mrs Hubback You've already had one.

Hubback There wasn't much left by the time it got to me. (*To Marisa*) Large g and t, please, Marisa.

Julian And the same for—(*He stops and looks at Agatha*) Is it all right if I have a drink?

Agatha Provided it doesn't take your mind off your work.

Marisa Two gee-and-tee?

Julian That's right—(*imitating her accent*)—two gee-and-tee.

Marisa starts to go

I'll come and help you.

Hubback So will I!

Hubback and Julian start to follow Marisa

Mrs Hubback Charles! I don't think it takes three people to pour two "gee-and-tee".

Julian No, of course it doesn't! Marisa and I can manage.

Julian grins triumphantly at Hubback, takes Marisa's arm and they exit quickly into the hall

Agatha remembers her poor, lost sister and her face crumbles

Agatha Poor Fiona. . . . I should never have let her out of my sight.
Mrs Hubback You *must* try not to worry, Agatha.

Hubback snorts at the use of Mrs Hepworth's first name

Agatha But she was my responsibility. She's stupid, you see, Audrey. Stupid. (*Crossing to the table* DR) Got no more brain than she was born with. She probably went off for a walk and lost her way.
Hubback If she's lost her way she'll go to the Police.
Agatha She'd never have the nerve to go to the Police. And if she did they'd probably arrest her! (*She sits*) If only she'd come walking in here now, I'd be *so* pleased to see her. . . . I mean, when all's said and done, she is my sister, isn't she?
Hubback Yes. And blood's thicker than water.
Agatha Well, you don't have to put it quite like that!
Hubback Oh. Sorry. (*He tries to cheer her up a bit*) Don't you worry. We'll find her. It's all under control.
Mrs Hubback Why? Do you have a plan of action, Charles?
Hubback Of course I've got a plan of action! You don't become a Brigadier without a plan of action.
Mrs Hubback All right, then. Explain it.
Hubback What?
Mrs Hubback (*patiently*) Explain your plan of action, Brigadier. (*Crossing to Agatha*) You'd like to hear about his plan of action, wouldn't you, Agatha?
Agatha Yes, I certainly would.
Mrs Hubback There you are, Charles.
Hubback Oh. Very well. Right.

Agatha and Audrey move the chairs round a bit, and sit side-by-side facing him

Hubback goes and collects his "baton" and piece of hardboard. We now see that on it is a large map of the area in various bright colours. He props it up on the end of the sofa and stands to one side of it, rather proudly, as if about to give a briefing to his men

There you are!

Agatha and Audrey look at it, blankly, then at each other. They shrug and look back again at the map

Recognize it?

They peer at it for a moment

Agatha Is it anyone we know?
Hubback (*patiently*) It's a plan of the area.
Agatha Oh. Oh, I see. Yes. Very nice.
Mrs Hubback Well, go on, dear.

Hubback points out one area with his stick

Hubback Now—all this is the sea.

Mrs Hubback Then why have you marked it in red?
Hubback (*flustered*) For the sake of clarity.
Mrs Hubback It hardly makes it clear if you mark the sea in red.
Agatha Unless it's the Red Sea.

Agatha and Audrey laugh

Hubback seethes

Mrs Hubback Yes. Rather misleading, I would have thought.
Agatha Blue would have been nice for the sea. . . .
Mrs Hubback Exactly what I thought, Agatha.
Hubback I've already used the blue for something else!
Mrs Hubback Then you shouldn't have done, Charles. If the sea was going to figure in your map it would have shown a degree of foresight to earmark the colour blue for that particular area. Don't you agree, Agatha?
Agatha Yes, I do, Audrey. I mean, the sea *is* blue, isn't it?
Hubback (*exploding*) I don't give a damn what colour the sea is!

They look at him in surprise

Mrs Hubback Charles, there's no need to get excited. I'm surprised you ever became a brigadier if you can't take a little criticism.
Hubback (*trying to control himself*) Look—do you want me to go on?
Mrs Hubback Yes, of course.
Hubback Very well. (*He turns back to the map and is about to indicate another area when . . .*)
Mrs Hubback We're only trying to keep you straight on the details.
Hubback (*patiently*) Look—I *know* the sea is blue.
Mrs Hubback Well, that's something, anyway.
Hubback But for the sake of this map the sea is red. All right?
Mrs Hubback All right, Charles. If that's the way you want it.

Hubback attempts to return to the map

It's inaccurate though.

The ladies try hard not to show their amusement at his pomposity

Hubback (*indicating*) This is the sea. (*He waits, expecting a further interruption. They are silent, so he proceeds*) This is the railway at the back of the village. And these bits marked in blue are the hills.
Mrs Hubback Ah! *That's* where the blue got to. . . .
Agatha They used to play a song about that at the Palais on a Saturday night.
Hubback (*stonily*) A song about what?
Agatha The Blue Hills of Pasadena.

Mrs Hubback hides her laughter in her hand

Hubback (*trying to continue*) This is the main road. From here to here.
Mrs Hubback It's bright yellow!

Hubback Yes.
Mrs Hubback I've never seen a bright yellow road before.
Agatha Except in *The Wizard of Oz*.

The ladies laugh

Hubback (*perservering*) And this is the line of huts down on the beach.
Agatha Now yellow would have been lovely for the beach. . . .
Hubback The beach is green!
Mrs Hubback How absurd.
Hubback Look . . . do you want me to explain this or not?
Mrs Hubback Yes, of course we do, Charles. I'm sorry. We'll try not to
    interrupt again.
Hubback (*indicating*) All this area is being combed by a group under a chap
    named Potter; over here are the chaps from the Miramare Hotel under
    Mr Phipps; and meeting up with them from the north is a group under Mr
    Humbolt.
Agatha And what about the men from the nudist club?
Hubback Oh, they'll be hanging out over here.
Mrs Hubback In the green sand.
Agatha Well, I only hope you persuaded them to put their clothes on. If
    Fiona sees that lot approaching she'll think she's gone to Heaven.
Hubback So we've got four prongs to the attack——
Agatha (*to Mrs Hubback*) The nudists won't like that!

Agatha and Mrs Hubback laugh, then control themselves

Agatha (*to Hubback*) Sorry, dear.
Hubback Four prongs to the attack—here, here, here. And down there at
    the bottom.
Mrs Hubback And where will *you* be, Charles?
Hubback I'll be in HQ, of course.
Mrs Hubback And where's that—the bar of the Miramare Hotel?
Hubback (*ignoring her*) Now, if everything goes according to plan, the
    group commanders—Potter, Phipps, Humbolt and Bottomley—will be
    back here within an hour and Miss Francis will be in the net.
Mrs Hubback You make her sound like a prawn.

Marisa comes in from the hall with a gin and tonic

Marisa One gee-and-tee.
Hubback (*gratefully*) Thank God for that . . .! (*He takes the drink hastily
    and swallows a large mouthful*)

Mrs Hubback returns her chair to its original position

Marisa (*picking up the map*) Ah! I did not know you were an artist.
Hubback What?
Marisa It is very modern. Very colourful.
Mrs Hubback Yes. It certainly is!

Marisa puts the map down on the seat UL

Julian enters from the glass doors, carrying Fiona's cardigan. He crosses C

Agatha (*gazing in alarm*) Where did you get that from?
Hubback (*looking guiltily at his drink*) Marisa brought it for me.
Agatha Not that! *That!*
Julian (*surprised by her tone*) This?
Agatha Yes! Where did you get it from?
Julian One of the men found it down by the sea. Why? Is it yours?
Agatha (*heavily*) No. It's not *mine*. . . .
Julian Oh. Right. Well, I'll leave it at the—(*He starts to go*)
Agatha (*rising*) Oh, no, you won't!

Julian stops

Julian What?
Agatha Give it to me!
Julian I thought you said it wasn't yours——
Agatha No, it isn't mine——
Julian Exactly, so I——
Agatha But I *want* it!
Julian You can't have it, if it isn't yours——
Agatha (*loudly*) Give it to me! (*She grabs the cardigan from the astonished Julian. She looks at it for a second, then clutches it to her bosom and emits a wail of anguish*)
Agatha Aaaaaaaah . . . ! (*She moves, miserably, to the sofa*)

They all gaze at her in surprise and crowd around her, concerned

Hubback		What on earth's the matter . . . ?
Mrs Hubback	(*together*)	Agatha, what's wrong?
Marisa		Are you all right, Mrs Hepworth?
Julian		I don't understand . . . !

Mrs Hubback quickly grabs her husband's drink. Hubback looks aggrieved at being robbed of his gin for a second time

Mrs Hubback Here—you have this! (*She puts one arm around Agatha and with the other holds the glass to Agatha's lips, forcing her to drink it*)

Hubback watches in horror as the whole of his drink disappears down Agatha's throat. Mrs Hubback hands the empty glass back to Hubback. Hubback looks at the glass despondently and hands it to Marisa. Agatha recovers from the effects of the gin and prepares to cry again. Julian sees her face begin to crumble and attempts to stop it

Julian It's all right, Mrs Hepworth! You can *have* the cardigan! I don't care who it belongs to! You can have it!
Agatha (*starting to cry again*) Aaaaah . . . !
Hubback Oh, my God . . . !
Mrs Hubback Agatha dear, you must try to stop. I know it's a nice cardigan. Very nice. But no cardigan is worth crying over.
Agatha (*miserably*) But it's not mine. . . .

Julian That doesn't matter! You can have it! I've given it to you! It's yours now!

Agatha No, it's not!

Julian Yes, it is!

Agatha No, it's not! It's *hers*!

Mrs Hubback Whose?

Agatha Fiona's! And you know what this means, don't you? It means she's dead! That's what this means—Fiona's dead!

Mrs Hubback (*calmly*) No, Agatha dear. She's not dead. She's just lost her cardigan.

Agatha (*continuing inexorably*) I tell you, she's lying dead somewhere out there in a foreign field! And it's all my fault!

Hubback		Now, now! You mustn't feel like that. ...
Marisa	(*together*)	I am sure she will turn up all right. ...
Mrs Hubback		You can't judge anything by a cardigan. ...
Julian		Don't blame yourself, Mrs Hepworth. ...

Agatha I'm a wicked, wicked woman! Whatever's happened to her, Audrey, it was all *my* fault. She didn't want to come out here in the first place. I made her! I said it was good for her.

Julian And you were right!

Agatha (*snapping*) You call this good for her?

Julian I was only trying to help ... (*He breaks away* R)

Agatha Nothing like this ever happened to her at Eastcliffe! It was me. I made her come out here to her doom ...! She was feeling ill this morning—and she hadn't even got a room to be ill in! And I took no notice. I made a sick woman go down on to the beach. I made her go out there to die!

Mrs Hubback Agatha dear, I'm sure she's not dead.

Agatha (*to Marisa*) You'd better call the Police.

Hubback We've already got a big search party out there——

Agatha (*sharply*) You call that a search party? A few dozen tourists and a handful of naked men? Run along, Marisa—you call the Police!

Marisa Very well.

Marisa goes quickly out to the hall

Agatha Maybe I drove her away with the things I said. I was unkind. I was cruel. I've got a cruel, unkind tongue, I know I have. But it's only meant in fun. And now I'm a murderess! That's what I am—a murderess! (*She cries*)

Mrs Hubback I think you'd better come and have a little lie-down. ...

Agatha I haven't got a room to have a lie-down *in*!

Mrs Hubback You can use *our* room.

Hubback (*quietly*) Can she?

Mrs Hubback After all, it's really *your* room, isn't it, Agatha?

Agatha Well—yes, Audrey, I suppose it is, in a way.

Mrs Hubback So come along——(*She puts an arm around Agatha and starts to lead her towards the stairs*) You can wash your face, and put your feet up, and you'll soon feel a lot better.

Agatha That's very kind of you, Audrey dear. I won't forget your kindness, I really won't.

Mrs Hubback And you can safely leave the men to look after everything here.

Agatha (*as they go*) I'm sorry I'm such a burden to you, but—(*beginning to cry*)—when I think of my poor dear sister somewhere out there——

Mrs Hubback You really mustn't distress yourself——

Agatha Today was the first time she'd ever worn this cardigan, you see. She got it specially for her holidays. And now—now she may never, ever wear it again——

Mrs Hubback There, there, there——

Mrs Hubback comforts Agatha, putting her arm around her shoulder. Agatha clutches the cardigan in tears, but as they depart—and without stopping or looking down at it—she smoothly picks up her small suitcase and takes it with her. They exit upstairs

Hubback looks wearily at Julian

Hubback You had to go and bring that bloody cardigan in!

Julian Well, *I* didn't know she was going to carry on like that, did I? I thought it was just lost property. (*He puts Agatha's chair back where it was, then has a sudden thought*) You don't suppose her sister *is* dead, do you?

Hubback I hope not, or we'll never hear the end of it.

The crackle of fireworks and the sound of bright Italian music is heard. Hubback wanders across to look longingly out into the garden

Hubback Seem to be starting up out there.

Julian Yes.

Pause

Hubback Good fun, I should think.

Julian Yes.

Pause

Hubback Pity she chose today to get lost.

Julian Yes.

Pause

Hubback Could at least have left it till tomorrow.

Julian Yes.

Another sombre pause. Julian glances towards the hall, has an idea and turns back to Hubback

Julian Shouldn't you be at HQ?

Hubback (*blankly*) Why?

Julian Well ... you are in charge.

Hubback (*remembering*) Ah. Yes. See what you mean. H'm.

Julian Well, go on, then!

Hubback Yes. Rather. Right. (*He starts to go, then stops*) What are *you* going to do?

Julian Oh, I ... I've got things to see to ... out there.

Hubback (*suspiciously*) Where?

Julian In the ... in the office.

Hubback H'm. Right. See you later, then.

Julian Yes.

Hubback exits reluctantly, through the glass doors, carrying his "baton"

Julian watches him go, smiles happily, and goes towards the archway calling

(*Quietly*) Marisa. ...

Julian exits into the hall

Hubback reappears. He looks around to make sure Julian has gone, grins and makes, triumphantly, for the archway

Hubback (*quietly as he goes*) Marisa. ... Marisa. ...

Hubback exits into the hall

The sound of music and fireworks is heard from time to time

Fiona and Mario come in through the glass doors. She has caught the sun, is happy and relaxed, and just a little unsteady on her feet. Mario is still in his cricket clothes, but has rolled up the bottoms of his trousers and is carrying his shoes. They both look extremely content

Fiona You see—what did I tell you? I bet nobody's even missed us.

Mario I thought maybe your sister would be looking for you.

Fiona Oh, no. Not Agatha. I bet she didn't even notice that I'd gone!

They sink on to the sofa, side-by-side, pleasantly tired

Oh, we *did* have a nice day, didn't we, Mario? You know—I've never been to a wine-tasting before.

Mario No—that is what I thought!

Fiona What do you mean?

Mario (*with a smile*) You were not supposed to *drink* the wine.

Fiona Why ever not?

Mario You *taste*-a the wine. Then you spit him out.

Fiona Spit him out! What a waste! I wasn't going to do that. (*She smiles, reflectively*) I must have swallowed a mouthful of about twenty different wines ...

Mario (*gazing at her, enraptured*) You are a *won*derful woman. ...

Fiona S'sh—Someone might come in.

Mario I do not care if the whole world comes in ... (*He holds his hands out to her, gently*) Your-a hands, please.

Fiona (*shyly*) Don't be daft ...

Mario Please.

Fiona reluctantly gives her hands to him

Now I kiss-a your hands.

Fiona (*giggling*) Don't you go getting any ideas, now! I haven't had all *that* much to drink.

Mario bends over her hands and kisses them lingeringly. Fiona is embarrassed

You foreigners are all the same. You don't half make a meal of it.

Mario (*looking up at her*) I want to ask you something.

Fiona Oh?

Mario *You* have no husband——

Fiona No.

Mario *I* have no wife. So——(*He goes abruptly down on to one knee in front of her*)

Fiona jumps up in surprise and looks down at him

You will be my wife! (*He grabs her firmly around the knees*)

Fiona totters unsteadily

Fiona (*calling out*) Ooh! Mario!

They collapse onto the sofa, Mario on top of Fiona

Mrs Hubback comes downstairs, heading for the glass doors. She sees the struggling mass on the sofa, and reacts, appalled

Mrs Hubback Mr Marcello!

Fiona pushes Mario away in alarm, causing him to fall face down on the floor. Mrs Hubback looks astonished, then she sees Fiona

Miss Francis! (*She crosses to Fiona, delighted to see her back*) Are you all right?

Fiona Oh, yes. He's quite harmless really.

Mrs Hubback I was not referring to Mr Marcello. I'm so glad to see you back again—safe and sound.

Fiona Oh, that's very nice of you. What a sweet thing to say. Wasn't that a sweet thing to say, Mario?

Mrs Hubback Mario?

Fiona (*giggling*) That's his name. (*She indicates Mario*)

Mrs Hubback I see . . . (*She looks at Mario*) You seem to spend your entire life face down on the floor.

Mario gets to his feet, grinning at her

Mario You are a——

Mrs Hubback Yes, I know!

Fiona Have you seen my sister anywhere?

Mrs Hubback You didn't *appear* to be looking for your sister. She's lying down—upstairs.

Fiona You mean they've found us a room?

Mrs Hubback No. But for the moment Agatha is in *our* room.

Fiona (*astonished*) In your room?

Mrs Hubback Number two-oh-five. I think you'd better pop up and tell her that you're here. And in the meantime *I* shall go down to HQ and tell my husband that he can now call off his dogs of war!

Mrs Hubback sweeps out majestically through the glass doors

Fiona looks puzzled, then moves to Mario and takes his arm

Fiona What's she talking about?
Mario (*with a shrug*) I do not know.

> *Julian comes in from the hall, carrying his clipboard, and sees them. He looks surprised*

Julian Good lord! You're back! Are you all right?
Fiona I've never felt better ...!
Julian Well, where the hell have you been?
Fiona I've been with Mario.
Julian Who's Mario?
Mario I am.
Fiona He is.
Julian What?! You've been with *him*?
Fiona Oh, we've had a lovely time, haven't we, Mario?
Mario We certainly have! She is a *won*derful woman...!
Julian (*gazing at them, unable to believe his ears*) Now I've heard every-thing. I'd better go and tell the Brigadier about this. He'll never believe it!

> *Julian goes out, quickly, through the archway*

The sound of bright Italian music is heard

Mario (*his eyes lighting up*) Ah ...! You hear the music? We will dance!
Fiona I haven't danced for years——
Mario Once you have danced, you never forget him.
Fiona I think I'm too tiddly. (*She giggles*) You'll have to hold on to me.
Mario Yes, that is what I *want* to do!
Fiona Ooh—you are a *won*derful man!

> *Fiona gives another giggle of delight as Mario whisks her quickly through the glass doors to the music*

> *Hubback comes in from the archway, talking as he arrives. Julian is behind him*

Hubback Well, this *is* a relief, Miss Francis. Delighted to know that you're back safe and sound and that nothing dreadful has—(*He stops, seeing there is nobody there*) Miss Francis ...! (*He searches, briefly*) Where are you? (*He turns back to Julian*) Are you playing games, Whittle? There's no sign of the bloody woman.

Julian also sees nobody there and looks about, puzzled

Julian Good Lord. ... (*He looks about*) I could have sworn she was here a moment ago. Arm-in-arm.
Hubback Arm-in-arm?
Julian With *him*.
Hubback With who?
Julian Mr Marcello.

Hubback (*astonished*) The manager?
Julian Yes.
Hubback (*doubtfully*) You saw Miss Francis arm-in-arm with the manager?
Julian Yes. I think they'd been drinking.
Hubback You're the one who's been drinking! You expect me to believe that Miss Francis was arm-in-arm with a sex-mad Italian?
Julian But I spoke to her! They were standing just there!
Hubback Nonsense. You must have been seeing things.
Julian I tell you she was here! I'll find her. You'll see. She can't have gone far. (*Calling*) Miss Francis ... (*He peers out of the glass doors*) Miss Francis! (*As he goes*) Where the hell are you?

Julian disappears into the garden

Agatha comes down the stairs. She is now wearing a rather elaborate dress of mourning black and is trying to put on a brave face

Agatha I suppose there's no sign of my sister?
Hubback Ah. No. Afraid not. Well—Whittle said he'd seen her, but you know how unreliable *he* is.
Agatha I just can't bear to think what's happened to her. I really can't ... (*She snuffles into her handkerchief*)
Hubback We'll find her. Don't you worry. Everybody's out there searching.
Agatha (*severely*) Everybody except *you*!
Hubback I beg your pardon?
Agatha Well, you're in *here*, aren't you? You're not out there. You're in here—in the comfort!
Hubback But this is my post. This is H.Q.
Agatha I thought H.Q. was in the Miramare Hotel?
Hubback Ah. Yes. Well, it's ... it's a mobile H.Q. And now I've moved it. Here.
Agatha (*moving towards the windows, sadly*) Oh, my sister ...
Hubback Who?
Agatha (*turning, sharply*) My sister!
Hubback Oh. Yes.
Agatha What can have happened to her? She's out there somewhere—all alone—frightened—unhappy—maybe even dead ...!
Hubback (*going to comfort her*) Now, now—we can't have that sort of talk, Mrs Hepworth—
Agatha (*continuing, inexorably*) I never dreamt this would happen. I never dreamt that I'd be going home on the plane with an empty seat beside me and poor Fiona travelling underneath in a box with all the luggage!
Hubback She's bound to turn up sooner or later—
Agatha (*glaring at him*) I never thought I'd see the day when a British Army officer turned his back on the enemy. (*She crosses below him to* C) Deserting the sinking ship, that's what *you're* doing. Leaving your men without a commander-in-chief. Just imagine what it's like out there now—a crowd of tourists and naked men wandering the town with nobody to keep them under control!

Losing his temper for a moment, Hubback goes to her quickly and seizes her firmly by the shoulders

Hubback Now, look here—*you're* the one who needs to be kept under control! (*He shakes her, roughly*)

Agatha I *beg* your pardon? (*Then she stops and gazes at him for a moment, remembering something, then speaks in a hushed voice*) Aaaah ... wait a minute now ...!

Hubback What's the matter?

Agatha I think I've remembered ...

Hubback Remembered? Remembered what?

Agatha It brought it all back to me ...

Hubback What did?

Agatha You grabbing hold of me like that and shaking me! It brought it all back ...

Hubback (*impatiently*) Brought what all back?

Agatha Where it was that we met before!

Hubback Look here—I told you—we've *never* met before. (*He moves away from her*)

Agatha (*smiling broadly*) Oh, yes, we have! I remember it clearly now. (*With relish*) Catterick Camp ...!

Hubback turns in horror

Hubback What?

Agatha Catterick Camp. It's in Yorkshire.

Hubback I know where it is!

Agatha (*going to him*) Well, that's where it was. ...

Hubback Where what was?

Agatha Where we met! You were in the Army Catering Corps.

Hubback (*blustering*) Catering Corps? Nonsense! I was in the Queen's Own.

Agatha (*beaming with joy*) Catering Corps! I know because I was working in the NAAFI at the time—and you chased me round the back of the cookhouse.

Hubback I did no such thing!

Agatha And not only once, either—you did it several times! You were insatiable! Don't you remember?

Hubback No, I do not! (*He escapes below her towards the sofa*)

Agatha Still, I expect I've changed a bit since then, eh? (*She grins, playfully*)

Hubback You must have done ...!

Agatha (*closing to him again*) Well, it *was* a long time ago, love. I was just a slip of a girl in those days ... (*She cuddles up to him, romantically*)

Hubback (*remembering*) Yes, you were, weren't you ...? (*He covers quickly*) No, you weren't!

Agatha Ah! You *do* remember!

Hubback Now, look here, Mrs Hepworth——!

Agatha And what's all this "Brigadier" bit, eh? You must have been promoted. You were only a sergeant then.

Hubback looks about to have apoplexy

Hubback A sergeant?! In the Catering Corps?! I was *not*!

Agatha Oh, yes, you were! I never forget a face. (*Thoughtfully*) Funny, though—I can't see Audrey as the wife of a cook sergeant, somehow . . .

Hubback (*without thinking*) No—she wasn't!

Agatha *What*?

Hubback (*with difficulty*) Well . . . Audrey's my *second* wife.

Agatha Oh, I see . . . So she doesn't *know* that you were in the Catering Corps?

Hubback No—of course she doesn't! Oh, my God . . . !

Agatha Fancy pretending to her that you were in the Queen's Own—*and* a Brigadier! Oo, you are naughty, Charlie! (*She squeezes him, playfully*)

Julian returns from the garden

Julian There's no sign of her out there. I can't think *where* she's got to.

Hubback extricates himself quickly from Agatha's grasp

Hubback (*crossing to Julian; abruptly*) Never mind all that! I want a taxi outside in ten minutes!

Julian A taxi. Right. (*He crosses to between Agatha and Hubback and then reacts*) Why? Are you going somewhere?

Hubback Yes. We're going to the airport.

Julian (*astonished*) You and Mrs Hepworth?

Hubback Me and Mrs Hubback!

Julian Oh, good! They've got a plane for you, then?

Hubback No, they haven't!

Julian So why are you going to the airport?

Hubback Well, I—er—, well I—er—, well I—er—

Agatha Are you going to lay another egg?

Julian But what will you do at the airport when there's no plane going to England?

Hubback We'll get on the first plane with two empty seats no matter *where* it's going!

Julian But I thought you said—

Hubback (*red-faced*) A taxi, Whittle!

Julian A taxi. Right.

Julian exits to the hall

Hubback Now, look here, Agatha—

Mrs Hubback (*off*) Charles!

Hubback (*jumping, nervously*) Aah!

Mrs Hubback strides in through the glass doors

Mrs Hubback You weren't out there.

Hubback Wasn't I?

Mrs Hubback You were supposed to be at H.Q.

Hubback Well, I was here!

Agatha (*smiling*) Yes, he was here—talking to me! Weren't you, Charlie?

Mrs Hubback looks at Hubback in surprise. He shakes

Mrs Hubback Charlie?

Agatha Oh, sorry. I forgot. You prefer to be called "Brigadier", don't you, Charlie?

Hubback glares at her, grabs his wife and pulls her, abruptly, towards the stairs

Hubback Come along, Audrey!
Mrs Hubback Where are we going?
Hubback To pack!
Mrs Hubback To pack? Why?
Hubback Because we're leaving for the airport in five minutes.
Mrs Hubback Oh, good! They've got a plane for us, then?
Hubback No, they haven't!
Mrs Hubback (*puzzled*) But you said we'd wait *here* till they got a plane for us. Why have you changed your mind?
Agatha (*quietly*) Wouldn't you like to know . . .! (*She grins at Hubback*)
Hubback Will you come and pack!
Mrs Hubback There's no need to shout. You're not on the parade ground.
Agatha No. Nor in the cookhouse.
Mrs Hubback (*to Agatha, puzzled*) Cookhouse?
Agatha (*innocently*) Oh—didn't your husband ever tell you? He used to be a wonderful cook.
Mrs Hubback (*astonished*) A *cook*? Charles, I never knew that.
Hubback Well, I—er—, well, I—er—, well, I—er—Oh, my God . . .!

He grabs his wife's arm and drags her, protesting, off up the stairs

Agatha watches them go, laughing at his discomfort

Marisa returns from the hall

Marisa Mr Whittle says the Brigadier and his wife are leaving, so now you and your sister will be able to move into your room.
Agatha (*remorsefully*) My sister . . . Oh, I forgot all about her for a minute . . . There I was, laughing and . . . Poor Fiona . . . I shudder to think what's happened to her . . . (*She sits on the sofa* DL)
Marisa (*to* R *of the sofa*) Oh, you must not worry. I am sure she is all right.
Agatha All right? She could be dead for all we know!
Marisa Of course she is not dead—
Agatha Well, she soon *will* be! (*Suffering suitably*) I bet she's lying somewhere, frightened and lonely—just calling out for me . . .
Fiona (*off*) Agatha! Are you there?

Agatha freezes

Long pause

Agatha (*hushed*) That was her voice. . . . (*She looks up towards heaven*) Perhaps she's come back to haunt me for my wickedness.

Fiona comes in through the glass doors

Fiona No, Agatha. I'm over here.

They turn and see her. Fiona is smiling happily, still mellow from the wine-tasting. Agatha gazes at her, her eyes wide in disbelief, and rises slowly

Agatha You're . . . you're not dead, then?
Fiona No, Agatha. Of course I'm not dead.

Pause

Agatha (*loudly*) Well, you ought to be ashamed of yourself!
Marisa You are all right, Miss Francis!
Fiona Yes, thank you, dear. I'm just a bit giddy. (*She sits at the table* DR)
Agatha Fiona Francis, where have you been?
Fiona Well, first of all I sat down on the beach——
Agatha You sat on the beach? We were all going mad with worry and you sat on the beach?
Fiona Well, it was such a lovely afternoon. I went for a paddle. I tucked my dress up in my knickers and walked for miles. (*Innocently*) You haven't all been looking for me, have you?
Agatha (*seething*) Not only us—the Police, Coast Guards, fishermen— nudists! Everyone bar the Camel Corps!
Marisa The Brigadier spent the whole afternoon looking for you.
Fiona Oh, is that what they were doing? I saw him and some other men rushing up and down, but I didn't like to call out. They looked so busy.
Agatha They were busy all right—looking for you!
Fiona I didn't know . . .
Agatha We could all have been enjoying ourselves, but thanks to you we've been carrying on like a lot of blooming bloodhounds.
Fiona I never thought that you'd be worried, Agatha.
Marisa Your sister was very upset.
Fiona (*surprised*) *Were* you, Agatha?
Agatha (*assuming an air of indifference*) No. No, of course I wasn't. . . . (*She turns away*)
Marisa She thought you might be dead.
Fiona *Did* you?
Agatha (*grudgingly*) Well, I didn't want you dying out here, did I? I didn't want a sister of mine making a spectacle of herself. There's a time and a place to die, and the time isn't now and the place isn't here!
Fiona (*looking at Agatha*) Well . . . fancy you being upset, Agatha.
Agatha (*avoiding her eyes*) I wasn't upset.
Marisa (*considerately*) Miss Francis, would you like me to get you a drink?
Fiona Oo—no, thank you, dear! (*She giggles*) I think I've had enough for one day.
Agatha (*crossing to Fiona suspiciously*) What did you say?

Fiona realizes what she has said and puts one hand to her mouth, giggling

Fiona I've never been to a wine-tasting before.
Agatha (*unable to believe her ears*) A wine-tasting?
Fiona Yes. That's where I've been this afternoon.
Agatha Tasting wine?

Fiona Well, that's what they *do* at a wine-tasting.

Agatha So all the time we were going mad with worry thinking what a horrible end you might have come to, you were sitting on your backside tasting wine?

Fiona And not just tasting it, either.

Agatha What?

Fiona Well, I didn't know you were supposed to spit it out! (*She laughs*)

Agatha I can't imagine what people thought. A middle-aged spinster from England sitting all on her own knocking back the vino like there was no tomorrow.

Fiona Oh, I wasn't on my *own*.

A beat

Agatha What did you say?

Fiona I said I wasn't on my own. Well, I wouldn't have known where to go if *he* hadn't been with me, now would I?

Agatha *He?* Don't tell me you've been picking up *men* at your time of life?

Mario enters through the glass doors

Agatha sees him. Mario smiles broadly. Fiona giggles and goes to him

Agatha Oh, my God! Not *him*?

Fiona Yes!

Agatha I might have known. (*Going to them*) I told you to go after *younger* women!

Mario But she is a *wonderful woman.

Agatha With all your "wonderful women" I'm surprised you find time to run this hotel at all.

Fiona We had such a nice time, didn't we, Mario?

Mario We certainly did. (*He puts his arm around her*)

Agatha looks at them for a moment, unable to believe her eyes

Agatha She'll never go to Eastcliffe again now! (*To Fiona*) You ought to be ashamed of yourself.

Fiona You said I might sit on the beach and meet my dream man. Well, I *did* and I *have*!

The Hubbacks come downstairs, clothes protruding here and there out of their hastily-packed suitcases and with other loose items of clothing under their arms

Hubback Oh, for heaven's sake, Audrey—don't hang about!

Mrs Hubback Whatever's the hurry? There's no plane for us, so why can't we pack our things properly?

Fiona (*to Agatha*) Are they going, then?

Agatha (*smiling, triumphantly*) Yes, love—they're going!

Hubback (*putting down his suitcase so he can fasten his tie*) Sorry we can't stay, everybody, but you know how it is. Got to rush, I'm afraid.

Agatha Oh, *what* a pity. Just when we had *so* much to talk about ... (*She grins at Hubback*)

Julian comes in from the hall, looking far from happy

Hubback Ah! Taxi waiting, Whittle?
Julian I hope so . . .
Hubback Never mind hope so what about know so?
Julian (*miserably*) Your taxi's the least of my problems, I can tell you. (*He sits, disconsolately, on the sofa*)
Agatha (*to Marisa*) What's the matter with him?

Marisa shrugs

Mrs Hubback Well, goodbye, Agatha dear. I hope you enjoy the rest of your holiday.
Agatha Thank you, Audrey—but the cricket won't be the same without you!
Mrs Hubback Oh, by the way—how did *you* know about my husband being a good cook?

Hubback starts to panic. Agatha looks at him with a smile

Agatha You'd better ask *him*. He can tell you all about it while you're waiting for your plane.
Mrs Hubback (*puzzled*) Charles . . . ?
Hubback (*to Marisa, hastily*) Ah—well—goodbye, Marisa!
Marisa Goodbye, Charlie!

Hubback bends to pick up his suitcase. Marisa is about to pinch his bottom, but he catches her.

Hubback Ah-ha! (*He faces the other way and bends down again*)

Agatha pinches his bottom

Aaah!

Mrs Hubback looks at him in surprise, not having seen what happened

Mrs Hubback Charles!
Hubback Ah—it was the sun—through that window—on my neck—Oh, my God . . . !

Hubback stumbles out into the hall in confusion. Mrs Hubback strides after him, heavily laden with luggage

Mrs Hubback (*as she goes*) Charles . . . ?
Agatha Right, then, Mr Whittle, we'll just move all our things up to our room and then we can come down and have a nice dinner, can't we? (*She and Marisa start towards the luggage*)
Julian (*unhappily*) No, you can't . . . !

Marisa and Agatha stop and look at him

Agatha What do you mean "no, we can't"?
Julian There won't *be* any dinner!
Fiona No dinner?

Agatha (*to Fiona*) Will you leave this to me? You didn't have dinner last night when there *was* dinner. (*To Julian*) What do you mean no dinner?
Julian (*with difficulty*) Well, you see ... the kitchen staff have gone on strike!

They all react

All What?
Julian They walked out this afternoon.
Agatha (*heavily*) Oh, great! Fine package holiday this turned out to be!
Julian Well, it's not *my* fault! (*Indicating Mario*) *He*'s supposed to be the manager!
Fiona He's right, Mario. You *are* the bloody manager.
Agatha (*to Mario*) Well, Mr bloody Manager? What have you got to say for yourself?
Mario (*shrugging*) I did not know about this.
Agatha No, I should think you didn't. You were too busy tasting wine with my sister.
Julian (*miserably*) This has been one of the worst days of my life——
Agatha It hasn't exactly been the gaiety of nations for me, either, Mr Whittle! (*Then a big smile spreads across her face*) But *I* don't mind.

The others look at her in surprise

All You don't?
Agatha No, of course not!
Julian You—you don't *mind* that the the kitchen staff are all on strike?
Agatha (*beaming*) Of course I don't mind. *We*'ll do all the cooking!

They all look astonished

Fiona (*not too keen*) Will we?

Agatha is now once again brimful of energy and enthusiasm

Agatha 'Course we will! It'll be just like the NAAFI again. I'll make out a roster for kitchen duty.
Julian (*aside to Marisa*) She will, too!
Agatha Marisa dear, you go and get me the hotel register. I want the names of all the residents.
Marisa But they are all at the carnival.
Agatha Well, it'll be a nice surprise for them when they get back!

Marisa shrugs at Julian and runs out into the hall

Fiona Come on, then, Mario.

Fiona and Mario start to go

Agatha And where do you think you're off to?
Fiona We were just going to have a dance.
Agatha Haven't you had enough excitement for one day? (*Relenting*) Oh, all right. But only *one*, mind! 'Cos I shall need you two in the kitchen.
Fiona Come on, Mario—quick—before she changes her mind!

Fiona and Mario move towards the glass doors

Agatha And here—!

Fiona and Mario stop

Don't you two go getting yourselves lost again.

Fiona (*giggling*) I don't care if we do!

Agatha Fiona—do remember you're not nineteen. The way you're going on, anyone would suppose you were thinking of getting married.

Fiona Don't you be so sure that I'm not!

Fiona and Mario go quickly out towards the music

Agatha turns, enthusiastically, to Julian

Agatha Oh, this really is going to be fun, isn't it, Mr Whittle?

Julian (*wretchedly*) But what about the carnival? There's singing and dancing out there.

Agatha Well, you can't have everything, can you, Mr Whittle?

Julian I haven't had *any*thing yet!

Marisa returns from the hall with the hotel register

Agatha sees her, then looks back at Julian, relenting a little

Agatha Well, I tell you what. ...

Julian (*hopefully*) Yes?

Agatha (*kindly*) Before we start work in the kitchen—*you* can have one dance, too.

Julian (*his face lighting up*) Can I? Can I really? Oh, *good*! (*With a big smile, he crosses towards Marisa*)

Agatha With *me*!

Julian turns to look at Agatha in alarm. Agatha, smiling broadly, advances towards him, purposefully. Marisa watches, laughing

Julian Oh, no ...!

Julian runs away from her. He is trying to make his escape, with a beaming Agatha pounding after him in hot pursuit, as the music swells and——

The CURTAIN *falls*

FURNITURE AND PROPERTY LIST

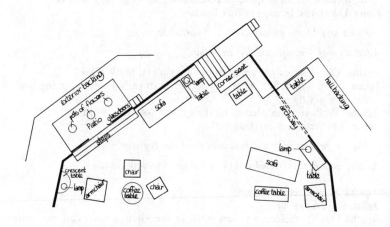

ACT I

SCENE 1

On stage: Two sofas. *On one:* Mrs Hubback's book
Two armchairs
Three low coffee tables. *On them:* magazines, travel brochures etc.
One crescent-shaped table
Two small tables
Three lamps
Upright chairs
Various pictures
Pots of flowers (on patio)

Off stage: Beach towel **(Marisa)**
Small suitcase. *In it:* plastic bag containing sequinned dress **(Agatha)**
Duty Free carrier bag **(Agatha)**
Tray 1. *On it:* pot of tea, milk jug, sugar, cup and saucer, spoon **(Marisa)**
Two suitcases. *In one:* washbag, various items of clothing **(Fiona)**
Small travelling grip **(Fiona)**
Carrier bag (full) **(Fiona)**

Brown paper parcel **(Fiona)**
Umbrella **(Fiona)**
Cup and saucer **(Marisa)**
Tray 2. *On it:* pot of tea, milk jug, sugar, cup and saucer, spoon **(Marisa)**
Clip board **(Julian)**
Sealed letter **(Agatha)**

Personal: **Hubback:** Binoculars
Agatha: Handbag. *In it:* pink travel document, passport, picture post-
cards, pen
Fiona: Handbag. *In it:* pill wrapped in tissue paper, sun glasses, pen
Julian: Courier's name tag

SCENE 2

Strike: 2 tea trays

Set: **Mrs Hubback's** book on table DR

Off stage: Sun-hat **(Agatha)**
2 Italian paper bags (full) **(Agatha)**
1 Italian paper carrier bag **(Fiona)** *In it:* Sun-hat
Bunch of flowers **(Marisa)**
Glass of gin and tonic **(Marisa)**
Small tray **(Marisa)**
Blanket **(Fiona)**
Pillow **(Fiona)**

ACT II

SCENE 1

Set: Folded blanket (sofa UC)
Pillow (sofa UC)
Agatha's luggage (near sofa UC)
Fiona's sun-hat (sofa DL)
Fiona's grip (near sofa DL)
Fiona's suitcase (on low table DL)
Cricket bat (corner seat)

Off stage: Beach towel **(Marisa)**
Beach towel **(Hubback)**
Beach towel **(Julian)**
Woman's Own **(Fiona)**
Cricket ball **(Mario)**

Personal: **Agatha:** Handbag. *In it:* Tube of brushless shaving cream, tube of lather
shaving cream

SCENE 2

Set: Paper decorations

Off stage: Hardboard with map painted on it **(Hubback)**
Wooden "baton" **(Hubback)**
Glass of gin and tonic **(Marisa)**

2nd glass of gin and tonic **(Marisa)**
Fiona's cardigan **(Julian)**
2 suitcases **(Hubbacks)**
Weekend-case **(Mrs Hubback)**
Loose items of clothing **(Hubbacks)**
Carrier bag **(Mrs Hubback)**
Handbag **(Mrs Hubback)**
Hotel register **(Marisa)**

Personal: Handkerchief **(Agatha)**

LIGHTING PLOT

Property fittings required: 3 table lamps

Interior. A hotel lounge. The same scene throughout

ACT I, SCENE 1.

To open: Bright summer sunshine

Cue 1	**Julian** sinks despondently on to the luggage *Black-out*	(page 21)

ACT I, SCENE 2

To open: Bright evening sunshine

Cue 2	**Fiona** covers herself with the blanket *Black-out*	(Page 39)

ACT 2, SCENE 1

To open: Bright summer sunshine

No cues

ACT 2, SCENE 2

To open: Twilight outside. Practicals on

No cues

EFFECTS PLOT

ACT I

Cue 1   As Curtain rises   (Page 1)
           Sound of cicadas in the trees, off. Fade out gradually when
           dialogue starts

ACT II

Cue 2   As Curtain rises   (Page 38)
           Sound of cicadas in the trees, off. Fade out gradually when
           dialogue starts

Cue 3   **Hubback:** "Or we'll never hear the end of it"   (Page 61)
           Sound of fireworks in the distance. Italian carnival music in the
           distance. Continue intermittently

MADE AND PRINTED IN GREAT BRITAIN BY
LATIMER TREND & COMPANY LTD PLYMOUTH
MADE IN ENGLAND